FivePoints
Learning

W9-APG-786

how to solve

SHSAT

SCRAMBLED
PARAGRAPHS

FIRST EDITION

STUDY GUIDE FOR THE NEW YORK CITY
SPECIALIZED HIGH SCHOOL ADMISSIONS TEST

STUYVESANT
BRONX SCIENCE
BROOKLYN TECH
STATEN ISLAND TECH

BROOKLYN LATIN
CITY COLLEGE
LEHMAN COLLEGE
YORK COLLEGE

· EXPERT STRATEGIES TO GIVE YOU THE EDGE ON THE TEST
· 100 SCRAMBLED PARAGRAPHS WITH EXPLANATIONS

HOW TO SOLVE
SHSAT
SCRAMBLED PARAGRAPHS
2012

HOW TO SOLVE SHSAT SCRAMBLED PARAGRAPHS 2012

By the Staff of Five Points Learning Test Prep and Admissions

FivePoints
Learning

New York

© 2012 by Five Points Learning, Inc.
Published by Five Points Publishing, a division of Five Points Learning, Inc.
1270 Broadway, Suite 1104
New York, NY 10001
E-mail: publisher@fivepointslearning.com

ISBN: 978-0-9859660-0-3

Publisher, Edward Song
Senior Editor, Noah Redfield
Editor, Justine Bottles
Editor, Brian Kirchner

Printed in the United States of America
10 9 8 7 6 5 4 3 2 1
August 2012

Five Points Publishing books are available at special quantity discounts. For
more information or to purchase books, please call our special sales department
at (212) 257 - 2264.

TABLE OF CONTENTS

FivePoints
Learning

—— INTRODUCTION

Ever hear the saying, "Practice makes perfect?" Well, we couldn't agree more. That's why we were shocked to discover that there are so few practice materials available for the strangest portion of the SHSAT: Scrambled Paragraphs.

Why are we afraid of spiders, snakes, or clowns? We're made to feel uncomfortable by anything unusual or unfamiliar, which is why spiders, snakes, and especially clowns get under our skin so easily. This is exactly why we're afraid of Scrambled Paragraphs.

We've been working with Reading Comprehension since 1st Grade. We may not like it, but we're certainly familiar with how it works. The same cannot be said for Scrambled Paragraphs. The only way to get comfortable with the format is to ***practice, practice, practice!***

And that's where we come in.

Once we've gone through the nuts and bolts of Scrambled Paragraphs, we'll launch you into our 100 practice paragraphs. We've divided them up into 20 practice tests presented exactly as you'll see them on the real SHSAT. We hope you enjoy working with us, and we wish you all the best.

Now, without further ado, let's jump in!

WHAT ARE SCRAMBLED PARAGRAPHS?

The SHSAT Verbal section begins with 5 Scrambled Paragraphs worth two points apiece. Each begins with a topic sentence followed by five supporting sentences that have been scrambled into the wrong order. All five sentences must be rearranged correctly in order to receive full credit.

HOW DO THEY WORK?

The five supporting sentences follow the topic sentence with the letters Q, R, S, T, and U. To the left of each letter is a line. Observe:

FivePoints
Learning

PARAGRAPH 1

Although quicksand has a frightening reputation, it is impossible to sink below one's waist.

_____ **Q.** It is best to use a walking stick to feel for this soft mixture before you find yourself trapped.

_____ **R.** This is because quicksand is formed from a mixture of sand, clay, and water, all of which combined is less dense than the human body.

_____ **S.** However, if you do find yourself trapped in quicksand, remain calm and do not try to fight your way out.

_____ **T.** Instead, lie back and spread your body across the surface in order to float.

_____ **U.** Once you are floating, swim slowly until you reach solid ground.

Use these lines to order the sentences from 1 to 5. That way, you can transfer the correct order to the answer grid more easily.

Speaking of which, let's take a look at a sample answer grid:

Paragraph 1					
The second sentence is	Ⓠ	Ⓡ	Ⓢ	Ⓣ	Ⓤ
The third sentence is	Ⓠ	Ⓡ	Ⓢ	Ⓣ	Ⓤ
The fourth sentence is	Ⓠ	Ⓡ	Ⓢ	Ⓣ	Ⓤ
The fifth sentence is	Ⓠ	Ⓡ	Ⓢ	Ⓣ	Ⓤ
The sixth sentence is	Ⓠ	Ⓡ	Ⓢ	Ⓣ	Ⓤ

Bubbling in the answers correctly is going to be a real pain unless you rank the sentences beforehand. **_Don't rely on your memory!_**

FivePoints
Learning

FINDING THE RIGHT ORDER: THE SIGNS

Let's say you're taking a cross-country trip from New York to Los Angeles. How do you know if you're going the right way? You follow the signs. What happens if you go to the mall and you're having trouble finding your favorite food court? You follow the signs. So how do you determine the right order for these Scrambled Paragraphs? *You follow the signs.*

There are five signs that you need to look for in every paragraph. *Find the signs, find the order.*

1. Transitions

Transitions indicate whether the sentence agrees with the rest of the paragraph or if it's changing gears instead.

Take another look at that quicksand paragraph and see if you can identify any transition words:

PARAGRAPH 1

Although quicksand has a frightening reputation, it is impossible to sink below one's waist.

_____ **Q.** It is best to use a walking stick to feel for this soft mixture before you find yourself trapped.

_____ **R.** This is because quicksand is formed from a mixture of sand, clay, and water, all of which combined is less dense than the human body.

_____ **S.** However, if you do find yourself trapped in quicksand, remain calm and do not try to fight your way out.

_____ **T.** Instead, lie back and spread your body across the surface in order to float.

_____ **U.** Once you are floating, swim slowly until you reach solid ground.

You should have spotted the words *although, however,* and *instead*. The topic sentence explains that *although* quicksand has a frightening reputation, it is impossible to sink to the bottom of a quicksand pit. **However,** if you are trapped in quicksand, don't try to fight your way out (S). **Instead,** spread your body out slowly (T).

FivePoints
Learning

Upon closer examination, "instead" in T must be referring back to S as it responds to the mistake of fighting quicksand with instructions on how best to handle the problem.

What we now know for sure is that S and T will be paired together in that order. We don't know where the pairing will fall in the paragraph yet, but we are one step closer to confirming the correct order of the five sentences. And that's based on one sign alone! Now, let's see how the other sentences will match up.

2. Repetition, Repetition, Repetition

If you can identify the repetition of names, places, actions, or objects, you may be able to further lock down the right order. Again: If you can identify the repetition of names, places, actions, or objects, you may be able to further lock down the right order. Once more with feeling: ***If you can identify the repetition of names, places, actions, or objects, you may be able to further lock down the right order.***

Let's go back to the wonderful world of quicksand and look for any repeating words.

PARAGRAPH 1

Although quicksand has a frightening reputation, it is impossible to sink below one's waist.

_____ **Q.** It is best to use a walking stick to feel for this soft mixture before you find yourself trapped.

_____ **R.** This is because quicksand is formed from a mixture of sand, clay, and water, all of which combined is less dense than the human body.

_____ **S.** However, if you do find yourself trapped in quicksand, remain calm and do not try to fight your way out.

_____ **T.** Instead, lie back and spread your body across the surface in order to float.

_____ **U.** Once you are floating, swim slowly until you reach solid ground.

For example, do you notice the words "float" and "floating" in sentences T and U, respectively? Take a look at the sentences in more detail. Which had to come first?

FivePoints
Learning

T instructs you to float while U explains what to do once you're floating, so logically, T comes before U. And we already know that S is before T let's put the letters together: **STU.**

Another repeating word is "mixture," found in Q and R. Let's scrutinize these sentences and find out one has to come first.

That's right: R must come before Q as it explains how the mixture works while Q merely refers to the mixture. Now, let's put these letters together: **RQ.**

Where is RQ most likely to fall: Before or after STU?

It's hard to say for sure. We need another sign.

Pronouns

Go back to R. To what is "this" referring? It calls back to the fact that one cannot sink below the waist in quicksand, which we learned in the topic sentence. Therefore, R has to be as close to the topic sentence as possible, meaning that the RQ pairing must be at the beginning.

Thanks to these three signs, we have the complete order: **RQSTU.** And that's your first Scrambled Paragraph complete. Congratuwelldone![1]

You already know that pronouns stand in for nouns. Use this to your advantage!

By way of another example, Q contains the phrase, "this soft mixture." The pronoun "this" indicates that some sentence came before, which was R because of the repetition sign. You will find many more paragraphs containing a plethora of pronouns to serve your unscrambling needs.

---

1   The authors acknowledge that "congratuwelldone" is not a real word. Still, it should be.

But enough about quicksand, let's talk about something a little more appetizing:

PARAGRAPH 2

The origins of pizza can be found in historical records dating all the way back to 1000 A.D.

_____ **Q.** Although American pizzerias already existed, this heightened demand helped make the Italian dish one of the most popular foods in the country.

_____ **R.** These pizzas were sold in Naples' market stalls, and were baked in ovens fueled by volcanic rock from nearby Mount Vesuvius.

_____ **S.** But the first pizzas resembling those we eat today appeared years later in Naples.

_____ **T.** These writings refer to a circle of cooked dough with a variety of toppings piled on top.

_____ **U.** During WWII, United States servicemen "discovered" pizza in Italy and wanted to see more of it when they returned home.

With a brand new paragraph comes a brand new sign.

Intro Words

Look out for anything that sounds like an introduction. Writers typically don't use intro words to finish off their paragraphs.

If sentence S is talking about **the first pizzas**, it's unlikely that the sentence will appear towards the end.

Say, why don't you try finishing the paragraph yourself? Remember to look for transitions, repetitions, and pronouns as well. You'll find the answers and explanations on page 12.

Let's take a look at one more paragraph:

PARAGRAPH 3

The rain barrel is now considered a viable method of water conservation.

_____ **Q.** This is because water can be gathered during the rainy season and then used during the dry season.

_____ **R.** While the water collected during the rainy season is not safe for drinking, it is excellent for gardening, landscaping, and cleaning.

_____ **S.** However, make sure that your barrels are properly secured and covered to keep any insects out.

_____ **T.** Moreover, rain barrels can store up to 150 gallons of unpurified water, so you won't need to use any drinking water for these activities.

_____ **U.** On a final note, remember to have your water tested before using it for gardening vegetables.

And with that, here's the fifth and final Scrambled Paragraphs sign.

Conclusion Words

Sometimes, they'll spell it out for you by writing, "in conclusion." Other times, words like, "and so," "finally" or "therefore" will tip you off that the sentence belongs at the end. Either way, keep an eye out for conclusion words. If writers don't use intro words at the end, it's unlikely that they'll insert conclusion words when they're first kicking off their paragraphs.

What's the one phrase in this paragraph that could only appear at the end? That is correct: ***On a final note.*** No matter what happens, sentence U must be involved in the wrap-up.

Now that you have all five signs in your lexicon, care to finish the paragraph? Remember to look up the answers and explanations on page 12.

FivePoints
Learning

RECAP

Transitions. Repetition. Pronouns. Intro Words. Conclusion Words.
The signs are always there in plain sight; you just need to look for them.
As you go through the 100 paragraphs, here are some extra pointers:

Basic Advice

- **DO THESE LAST!** Again, you've done Reading Comprehension a billion times in school, so why not stay within your comfort zone and do those first? Save the headache until the end. As the test is not in order of difficulty, you should focus on getting as many raw points as possible in the simpler sections. Reading, Logical Reasoning, and then Scrambled Paragraphs is the **safest** order for the Verbal.
- **WORK SLOWLY!** Speeding through the test will not guarantee a high score; if anything, you're more likely to make one careless mistake after another. The slower you work, the more points you will rack up. ACCURACY OVER SPEED.
- **WRITE EVERYTHING DOWN!** Scrambled Paragraphs are complicated enough without trying to juggle everything mentally. By constantly taking notes, you decrease the chances of becoming confused and messing up the order. GET OUT OF YOUR HEAD; IT'S A BAD NEIGHBORHOOD.
- **TRUST YOUR INSTINCTS!** Some of these paragraphs will be tougher than others. The signs are your best and only tools, but if you're still having trouble, go with your gut. Don't be afraid to guess.

And Finally...

- **RELAX!** If you wind up in panic mode, you won't be able to think clearly or work effectively. Stay positive, have faith in yourself, and try your best.

Any questions? Nope? Then I present you with your paragraphs. Good luck!

FivePoints
Learning

—— ANSWERS & EXPLANATIONS

PARAGRAPH 1 (RQSTU)

The topic sentence debunks the common myth that quicksand sucks its victims underneath the ground. R then explains why it is a myth and describes what components make up quicksand (a mixture of sand, water, and clay). Q links to R with the warning that it is best to use a walking stick to feel for "this soft mixture" before you find yourself stuck in the quicksand. S changes gears with "however" and explains what not to do if you're trapped in quicksand. T then explains how you should position yourself in order to float. U leads with "Once you are floating," and concludes with the victim reaching solid ground.

PARAGRAPH 2 (TSRUQ)

The topic sentence introduces the first records of pizza in 1000 A.D. T elaborates on these historical references. S transitions into the pizzas we eat today and declares the origin city Naples. R must follow as it elaborates on its place in the Naples marketplace. U states that U.S. Servicemen "discovered" pizza while in Italy and wanted more of it back in the United States. Q gives the effect of "this heightened demand," which was to make pizza one of the most popular foods in the country.

PARAGRAPH 3 (QRTSU)

The topic sentence introduces rain barrels as a popular way to conserve water. Q explains why this is a viable method and summarizes how the process works. R states that the water is not safe for drinking but is useful for the other listed activities. T starts with "moreover," a transition that agrees with the previous sentence, and elaborates on why you don't need to use the water for drinking. S changes gears with the word "however" and reminds the reader to make sure the barrels mentioned in T are properly secured. U leads with, "On a final note," which can only be the paragraph's concluding sentence.

Scrambled Paragraphs
Tests 1-20

———————— TEST ONE

PARAGRAPH 1

When Yuri Gagarin was a little boy, space travel was just a concept found in science fiction.

_____ **Q.** As a cosmonaut, Gagarin became the first person to orbit the Earth.

_____ **R.** Thus, Yuri Gagarin took the first small step toward transforming space exploration from fiction to reality.

_____ **S.** But when he was a young man, Gagarin began his training to become a cosmonaut, which is the Russian term for astronaut.

_____ **T.** He undertook this voyage in a spacecraft called the Vostok 1, which contained just enough room for himself and all the bare necessities for his survival.

_____ **U.** Surprisingly, he didn't return inside the Vostok 1, but instead ejected from his compartment and landed in Russia via parachute.

PARAGRAPH 2

The legend of El Dorado has ignited the imaginations of explorers and dreamers for centuries.

_____ **Q.** Supposedly made entirely of gold, El Dorado was rumored to span throughout South America and along the Amazon River.

_____ **R.** It is no wonder that El Dorado is now used figuratively to denote a dream or desire.

_____ **S.** Some explorers also found several gold pieces in Lake Guatavita where the natives had thrown their valuables to appease the gods.

_____ **T.** This legend, for which so many died, partly originates from a tribe in the Andes who would cover their new chieftains with gold dust.

_____ **U.** Countless explorers and adventurers stopped at nothing to find this mythical city of gold, only to lose their lives in the process.

FivePoints
Learning

PARAGRAPH 3

The beautiful but poisonous lionfish has caused extensive damage to Florida's delicate marine ecosystem.

_____ Q.   When Hurricane Andrew struck, six lionfish escaped from the Pacific and Indian Oceans, and found their way into the Atlantic Ocean.

_____ R.   These fish multiplied rapidly and, without any predators to threaten them, have been attacking whole species of marine life ever since.

_____ S.   Today, scientists and local environmentalists are searching for ways to control the lionfish population and return order to the waters.

_____ T.   As a result, lionfish continue to threaten not only the commercial fishing industry but also the ecological balance of this ecosystem.

_____ U.   Among their prey are herbivores found in commercial fisheries that help sustain coral reefs by consuming excess seaweed.

PARAGRAPH 4

An orchestra conductor's job is far more involved than one realizes.

_____ Q.   All these elements come together to weave the fabric of every performance.

_____ R.   For example, the conductor is usually responsible for recruiting and hiring performers to build a strong orchestra.

_____ S.   Finally, he/she conducts the music by controlling the tempo, dynamics, and time of each performance using precise arm movements.

_____ T.   The conductor must then study these selected pieces and learn each score by heart so he knows all the appropriate cues for the musicians.

_____ U.   Another important job is to choose the works that will be performed by the orchestra that season.

FivePoints
Learning

PARAGRAPH 5

The FIFA World Cup is the most popular sporting event in the world.

_____ **Q.** Only 8 of these teams have won the World Cup with Brazil's bringing the trophy home more than that of any other nation.

_____ **R.** In addition to fostering a competitive spirit, the World Cup unites disparate nations by promoting fair play and global mutual respect.

_____ **S.** Only 13 teams participated in that first tournament, but nowadays, a total of 32 teams compete for the coveted title.

_____ **T.** The first official World Cup took place in Uruguay in 1930 and has since been held every four years at a different location around the globe.

_____ **U.** This event brings the world's best soccer teams together to compete against each other for the title of World Champion.

———————— TEST TWO

PARAGRAPH 1

Ants have an astonishing ability to communicate with their colonies through a chemical release.

_____ **Q.** Ants also use this scent to identify members of their own nest, ensuring that intruders do not steal their eggs or larvae.

_____ **R.** Chemoreception is a process by which ants secrete chemicals called pheromones that leave off an aroma that other ants can detect.

_____ **S.** This type of communication is called chemoreception.

_____ **T.** The survival of ant communities depends on effective and orderly systems such as this communication method.

_____ **U.** In doing so, they leave behind a pheromone trail that enables the ants to retrace their steps and allows others from the colony to follow their lead.

PARAGRAPH 2

Viruses are microscopic organisms that attach themselves to cells and infect the body through a process called the lytic cycle.

_____ **Q.** Each virus is made up of set of genetic instructions called Nucleic acids.

_____ **R.** Once the host is infected, the particles break free and attack other cells, thereby restarting the lytic cycle.

_____ **S.** Coats of protein not only protect the acids but also allow them to feel and recognize a host cell.

_____ **T.** The virus then infiltrates the host cell, using it as a home as well as a breeding ground to replicate into other virus particles.

_____ **U.** A lipid membrane that surrounds the protein is used to attach the virus to the host cell.

FivePoints
Learning

PARAGRAPH 3

Anna Mary Robertson, also known as Grandma Moses, began her painting career at the age of 76.

_____ **Q.** She sold her first paintings at a local county fair and displayed others at her local drugstore.

_____ **R.** Afterwards, Grandma Moses became a household name and went on to produce over 1,000 works before her death at 101.

_____ **S.** One day, vacationing art dealer Louis Caldor stepped into the drugstore and bought up her entire collection.

_____ **T.** She remains one of the most famous American folk artists of the 20th century.

_____ **U.** Caldor showcased her works in an exhibition at the Museum of Modern Art.

PARAGRAPH 4

As the ancient Roman Republic expanded, local governments realized they needed an efficient system to provide clean water to their townspeople.

_____ **Q.** Nevertheless, the aqueducts proved a great source of water until the fall of the Roman Empire in 400 AD.

_____ **R.** Engineers designed these aqueducts with a slope as a means to transport the water into the cities.

_____ **S.** Each slope had to be just right: one that wasn't steep enough would keep the water stranded, whereas one that was too steep would result in flooding.

_____ **T.** Their solution was the aqueduct, a bridge-like structure that transports large amounts of water from a remote source.

_____ **U.** Adding to this challenge was the fact that some aqueducts were built above ground while others were constructed below ground.

FivePoints
Learning

PARAGRAPH 5

The Internet is a worldwide network linking every connected computer to its interface.

_____ **Q.** Despite its lack of complete ownership, the internet is overseen by several organizations that make sure these protocols are up to date.

_____ **R.** Since the Internet isn't owned by a single entity, it is governed by rules known as protocols designed to oversee the Internet's infrastructure.

_____ **S.** The interface enables ownership of various pieces of the internet, although nobody can ever own the internet as a whole.

_____ **T.** An example of one of these pieces would be an Internet Service Provider (ISP), a business that charges money for a connection.

_____ **U.** The experts within each group do their part to maintain the internet's integrity.

FivePoints
Learning

—————— TEST THREE

PARAGRAPH 1

Mark Twain is one of the finest and most cherished literary icons in American history.

_____ **Q.** After the river trade stalled due to the Civil War, Twain returned to newspaper writing and soon gained national recognition for his work.

_____ **R.** After the death of his father, Clemens left school to become a printer's apprentice and then worked at his brother's newspaper.

_____ **S.** He was born Samuel Clemens and grew up on the Mississippi River.

_____ **T.** He went on to write 28 books, most notably *The Adventures of Tom Sawyer* and *The Adventures of Huckleberry Finn*.

_____ **U.** Then, as a teenage river pilot's apprentice, Clemens used the code for, "safe to navigate," to create a new pen name: Mark Twain.

PARAGRAPH 2

Domestic pigs quickly become feral when released into the wild.

_____ **Q.** This ability to change characteristics based on environment is called phenotypic plasticity.

_____ **R.** Once in the wild, the pigs must adapt to their new surroundings in order to survive.

_____ **S.** One new characteristic is denser, coarser, and longer hair that lends an extra layer of protection for the pigs.

_____ **T.** The swine also grow tusks and become more aggressive to further protect themselves.

_____ **U.** Within a few months, the changes are complete and the feral pig bears little resemblance to its domestic counterpart.

FivePoints
Learning

PARAGRAPH 3

King Nebuchadnezzar II built the Hanging Gardens of Babylon in 600 BC.

_____ **Q.** The completed gardens so astonished all who saw them that they were once regarded as among the Seven Wonders of the Ancient World.

_____ **R.** Her gardens were layered terraces that resembled an artificial mountain.

_____ **S.** They also included hollow pillars that held up each level and from which grew a multitude of trees.

_____ **T.** Amytis came from a lush, mountainous region and therefore disliked the dry Mesopotamian terrain.

_____ **U.** These magnificent gardens were built to comfort the king's homesick wife, Queen Amytis.

PARAGRAPH 4

Benjamin Banneker was an African-American astronomer, surveyor, and mathematician.

_____ **Q.** His astronomical abilities were such that he correctly predicted the time and date of a solar eclipse.

_____ **R.** He later went on to publish a Farmer's Almanac, which took him five years to complete.

_____ **S.** This son of a former slave also left his stamp on American history by using his great intellect to put forth some of the earliest arguments against slavery.

_____ **T.** Naturally, Banneker calculated all of the information included in the Almanac himself.

_____ **U.** His surveying career came about when George Washington appointed Banneker to a committee that mapped the boundaries of Washington DC.

FivePoints
Learning

PARAGRAPH 5

Aquaponics is the combination of aquaculture and hydroponics.

_____ **Q.** The cycle begins when fish are stored in tanks or containers.

_____ **R.** As the waste from the fish is rich in nutrients, the water acts as a liquid fertilizer for the plants.

_____ **S.** The clean water then returns to the fish tank so the cycle can begin again.

_____ **T.** The plants are housed in hydroponic beds that extract the nutrients, thereby preventing the water from turning toxic.

_____ **U.** It involves the cultivation of plants and aquatic animals in a mutually beneficial environment.

FivePoints
Learning

—————— TEST FOUR

PARAGRAPH 1

The South African Stiletto snake is known for its strange features and clever hunting techniques.

_____ **Q.** Its name refers to the snake's thin fangs that resemble stiletto blades.

_____ **R.** This flexibility is useful for the reptile to covertly attack from underground.

_____ **S.** The fangs are retractable, and since their mouth muscles push them forward, they do not need to open their mouths to attack.

_____ **T.** After biting its prey, the snake's fangs return to their horizontal position until the next time the snake needs to eat.

_____ **U.** Once a target is spotted, the snake rises from its underground lair to mount an attack.

PARAGRAPH 2

The Bering Land Bridge was one of the ancient world's greatest crossroads.

_____ **Q.** The bridge was named after Vitus Jonassen Bering, a Russian Naval officer who led two expeditions across the bridge in the early 18th century.

_____ **R.** Anthropologists continue to study the area as it holds much of North America's earliest history.

_____ **S.** This enabled people to migrate to North America and establish colonies and cities.

_____ **T.** But the bridge actually formed during the last ice age when a series of natural disasters occurred between Asia and North America.

_____ **U.** In time, a 1,000-mile wide stretch of land linked the two continents.

FivePoints
Learning

PARAGRAPH 3

Plato was the first to describe Atlantis after he heard an Egyptian legend of the lost underwater city.

_____ **Q.** Perhaps further excavation will put an end to this 2,000-year-old mystery.

_____ **R.** He described an island and a near perfect civilization that suddenly sank to the bottom of the sea due to a natural disaster.

_____ **S.** In fact, recent satellite photos of Southern Spain show that a flood destroyed part of its coast just a few hundred years before Plato's writings.

_____ **T.** The photos show remnants of structures similar to the palaces described by Plato.

_____ **U.** But recent speculation states that the Egyptian word for "coastline" was confused with their word for "island."

PARAGRAPH 4

In Ancient Japan, samurai wielded significant military and political power.

_____ **Q.** But shortly after the Meiji Restoration, the new emperor created a national army and did away with the samurai.

_____ **R.** As samurai followed a strict code of honor called the bushido, they valued honor and loyalty to their masters above all else.

_____ **S.** These warriors were hired by wealthy feudal lords to protect their families and their land.

_____ **T.** In addition, the warriors fought on horseback and wore full body armor in battle.

_____ **U.** The first samurai were archers, but they later became known for their sword-fighting skills.

FivePoints
Learning

PARAGRAPH 5

Hurricanes are fierce storms that evolve in tropical regions surrounding the equator.

_____ **Q.** Since hurricanes usually form weeks before hitting land, forecasters have plenty of time to recommend evacuations and hopefully save lives.

_____ **R.** Also known as typhoons, these storms can reach speeds up to 185 miles per hour.

_____ **S.** Hurricane season begins June 1st in the Northern Hemisphere and lasts until the end of November.

_____ **T.** They can also cause the ocean to swell upwards of 50 feet.

_____ **U.** During this season, meteorologists carefully study tropical storms for signs of wind increase in order to predict a Hurricane early on.

FivePoints
Learning

TEST FIVE

PARAGRAPH 1

In 1792, two-dozen men met under a buttonwood tree to discuss business security reforms.

_____ **Q.** These men created the Buttonwood Agreement, which established the basis for the New York Stock Exchange.

_____ **R.** The Exchange eventually moved to a street between the banks of the Hudson River and the East River.

_____ **S.** Wall Street was named after the twelve-foot stronghold that Dutch settlers built a century before.

_____ **T.** While there is no longer a wall on Wall Street, the name still reminds us of the area's eclectic history.

_____ **U.** The settlers built the wall in order to protect themselves from intruders.

PARAGRAPH 2

The Mexican revolutionary Francisco "Pancho" Villa was born into poverty in the state of Chihuahua.

_____ **Q.** He later became an icon of the Mexican Revolution, spending so much time on horseback that he became known as the "Centaur of the North."

_____ **R.** Thanks to Gonzalez, Villa abandoned his old ways and dedicated himself to fighting for human rights.

_____ **S.** These circumstances led him to a career as a bandit before meeting a man who would change his life.

_____ **T.** A local political figure named Abraham Gonzalez educated Villa about the government's power to affect the lives of its people.

_____ **U.** Despite Pancho Villa's assassination, he retains his iconic status in Mexican history.

FivePoints
Learning

PARAGRAPH 3

Great herds of buffalo once roamed the American West.

_____ **Q.** Native Americans used every part of the buffalo for survival, and hunted only when their tribes needed food.

_____ **R.** There is only one significant herd of buffalo left and scientists are working tirelessly to rebuild their community before it's too late.

_____ **S.** The buffalo first migrated from Asia to North America back when the Bering Land Bridge connected the two continents.

_____ **T.** But the white settlers of the 1800s killed buffalo by the hundreds of thousands and did so only for profit.

_____ **U.** By the end of the century, all but a few thousand buffalo were killed.

PARAGRAPH 4

The North Pole Environmental Observatory was established to allow an international research team to perform annual expeditions.

_____ **Q.** When the time comes, the expedition sets up camp in the North Pole to study how the sea regulates the world's climate.

_____ **R.** These recordings are managed by attaching various instruments to a mooring line, which the team submerges into the ocean.

_____ **S.** They do this by sampling the waters of the Arctic Ocean and keeping records of salt measurements, sea temperatures, and ice depth.

_____ **T.** Divers must also explore the icy waters themselves to obtain further data.

_____ **U.** The expedition is supported by the National Science Foundation and continues to enlighten the scientific community on our northernmost ocean.

FivePoints
Learning

PARAGRAPH 5

The Colossus of Rhodes stood 110 feet tall and was built after the defeat of General Demetrius and his army.

_____ **Q.** When Demetrius retreated, he left behind several war machines, which provided the necessary material to construct the bronze statue.

_____ **R.** When the remains of the Colossus were sold a few centuries later, it allegedly took 900 camels to transport all of the pieces.

_____ **S.** The finished statue stood at the entrance of the Mandraki harbor until an earthquake proved to be its undoing.

_____ **T.** Chares situated the statue on stone columns that stood fifty feet high and were attached to iron beams.

_____ **U.** Its construction was left under the command of Chares, a prominent sculptor who would finish it 12 years later.

FivePoints
Learning

———— TEST SIX

PARAGRAPH 1

Mount Everest, the tallest mountain in the world, is part of the Himalayan mountain range.

_____ **Q.** Then it was renamed when British surveyor George Everest was the first to measure the mountain.

_____ **R.** As technology improved, geographers and mountaineers petitioned for the mountain to be measured a second time.

_____ **S.** Thus, a team of scientists re-measured Everest's elevation using two Global Positioning System receivers.

_____ **T.** These new measurements put the mountain at 8,850 meters, almost two meters taller than those previously recorded.

_____ **U.** Its former name was Chomolungma, which means, "goddess of the universe."

PARAGRAPH 2

During the Age of Exploration, Spain sent conquistadors to explore new lands and claim them for the country.

_____ **Q.** He landed on the island of Puerto Rico, and founded the first settlement of which he was bestowed the title of Governor.

_____ **R.** After sailing with Christopher Columbus on his second journey to the new world, Leon decided to set out on his own when they returned to Spain.

_____ **S.** After two years, a new governor was appointed and his men sailed to colonize Florida.

_____ **T.** One such conqueror, Ponce de Leon, explored Florida and the adjacent Caribbean islands.

_____ **U.** This would be Leon's last journey, for when the native Calusa people attacked him, it was at the cost of his life.

FivePoints
Learning

PARAGRAPH 3

Geocaching is a modern day scavenger hunt using grid coordinates and a GPS.

_____ **Q.** Each location is rated between one and five stars to help people choose an appropriate level of difficulty.

_____ **R.** The grid coordinates can be accessed online along with a brief description of the location as well as the difficulty level of the findings.

_____ **S.** Once a location is chosen, the grid coordinates lead the seeker to a site where a geocache is hidden along with a small treasure and a logbook.

_____ **T.** The logbook is then signed and the geocache is returned to its exact hiding spot.

_____ **U.** After the geocache is located, he claims the treasure and replaces it with a new one for the next adventurer.

PARAGRAPH 4

Origami is the ancient art of paper folding.

_____ **Q.** This art form is a traditional part of Japanese culture; animals, flowers, and boxes are the most common designs today.

_____ **R.** Books like _Window on Midwinter_ made origami accessible to everyone and turned origami into a popular pastime in Japan.

_____ **S.** One such book, _Window on Midwinter_, provided approximately 150 of these models.

_____ **T.** Initially, origami techniques were passed down by word of mouth for many generations leaving many styles of folding a mystery.

_____ **U.** In order to solve this issue, a series of writers compiled directions for various origami models.

PARAGRAPH 5

The most famous of the Ancient Egyptian pyramids is Khufu's Great Pyramid of Giza.

_____ **Q.** The arduous task of constructing the pyramids was nearly as awe-inspiring as the structure itself.

_____ **R.** Between 20,000 and 30,000 men worked on the Pyramid of Giza for more than 80 years using stone blocks.

_____ **S.** This amazing structure continues to draw tourists from all over the globe.

_____ **T.** It is listed as one of the Seven Wonders of the World for its size as well as its architectural genius.

_____ **U.** Standing 481-feet tall, it was the tallest building in the world for almost 2,000 years until the Eiffel tower was built in 1889.

TEST SEVEN

PARAGRAPH 1

Community barn raisings were common during the 18th and 19th centuries.

_____ **Q.** During this time, barns were necessary for a family's survival because they housed cattle and grain during the winter months.

_____ **R.** For example, when a new family moved into the area, the entire community pitched in and built the barns in just a few days.

_____ **S.** Participation wasn't optional; everyone was required to help.

_____ **T.** In addition, barns helped new families establish interdependence and strengthen their communities.

_____ **U.** Because of their collaborative efforts, many of these barns still stand today.

PARAGRAPH 2

Nat Love, also known as Deadwood Dick, is a notable African-American cowboy of the Old West.

_____ **Q.** Once freed, Nat headed to Dodge City, Kansas and began working for the Duval family after he successfully tamed the wildest horse on the ranch.

_____ **R.** While working on the Duval ranch, Nat was given the nickname Deadwood Dick.

_____ **S.** The South Dakota town Deadwood gave him the name after Nat won every single event in a Fourth of July rodeo.

_____ **T.** Deadwood Dick's life of adventure and bravery continues to embody the spirit of the American Cowboy.

_____ **U.** Nat was born a slave in Tennessee and was freed at the end of the Civil War.

FivePoints
Learning

PARAGRAPH 3

Although the leafy seadragon is named for the mythical creature, it is a genuine aquatic creature.

_____ Q. Nevertheless, the leafy seadragon is on the Near-Threatened Species list and is therefore protected by the Australian government.

_____ R. While it does bear a slight resemblance to dragons, it is actually a species of seahorse.

_____ S. These appendages provide the seahorse with an excellent source of camouflage.

_____ T. At first glance, you might think a leafy seadragon is covered in seaweed because of its orange, green, and gold appendages.

_____ U. Also known as the Australian seahorse, this unique creature can only be found on the Western shoreline of Australia.

PARAGRAPH 4

The catapult is a wooden siege engine and used throughout much of Europe and China.

_____ Q. Although catapults proved useful in ancient battle, the invention of gunpowder eventually rendered them obsolete.

_____ R. In order to achieve this, the catapult was designed to support weight on one end of its seesaw-like design.

_____ S. When constructing a catapult, a large sling or basket is attached to one end of a wooden arm with a counterweight attached to the other.

_____ T. Catapults are perhaps best known for their use in medieval times as an effective method of hurling items over castle walls.

_____ U. This basket is then pulled down and released, causing the weighted arm to slam to the ground and launch the projectile towards its target.

FivePoints
Learning

PARAGRAPH 5

The Supreme Court is the head of the United States judicial branch.

_____ **Q.** The Supreme Court only rules on approximately 150 cases of the thousands requested each year.

_____ **R.** It can also decide if a president or any level of government is acting in an unconstitutional manner.

_____ **S.** Congress created the court to interpret whether or not certain laws should be in place.

_____ **T.** Nine justices, who are appointed for life by the President of the United States, oversee these cases.

_____ **U.** The Supreme Court's rulings are final, and there is no court in the country that will hear a further appeal.

—————— TEST EIGHT

PARAGRAPH 1

The world's first space-based optical telescope is the size of a school bus and weighs almost as much as two elephants.

_____ **Q.** The enormous Hubble telescope is also solar powered and has two 25-foot solar panels along the surface of the instrument.

_____ **R.** This $1.5 million dollar telescope collected its first image, a star cluster, on May 20, 1990.

_____ **S.** Moreover, it contains a set of nickel-hydrogen batteries that are used to run the telescope's power.

_____ **T.** All of this data is then stored on magneto-optical disks, thus providing NASA with invaluable information about our Solar System.

_____ **U.** Today, the Hubble collects 120 gigabytes of space data every week, which is the storage equivalent of three Empire State Buildings.

PARAGRAPH 2

The Platypus is an unusual animal because of its appearance and its physical traits.

_____ **Q.** One of its most significant qualities is that it lays eggs rather than gives birth.

_____ **R.** All of these features allow the platypus to navigate on land as well as under water.

_____ **S.** For example, male platypuses have spurs located on their hind feet that inject venom into predators and prey alike.

_____ **T.** The platypus is also one of the few venomous mammals in existence.

_____ **U.** Other significant traits include webbed feet, a duck-like bill, and a beaver-like tail.

FivePoints
Learning

PARAGRAPH 3

Aristotle provided an invaluable education to a young Alexander the Great.

_____ **Q.** As king, Alexander conquered the Persian and Greek Empires before his death from fever at the age of 33.

_____ **R.** Aristotle's teachings enabled Alexander to become one of the greatest conquerors of all time.

_____ **S.** When his father died, Alexander went from captain to king of Macedonia.

_____ **T.** During this time, he quickly gained the respect of his soldiers for his sharp mind and unrelenting bravery.

_____ **U.** For instance, after his formal schooling was complete, Alexander became a captain of the Macedonian army.

PARAGRAPH 4

Japan's Shinkansen, or "bullet train," is the very first of its kind.

_____ **Q.** In addition, this new version of the train is known for its reliability and speed.

_____ **R.** The original Shinkansen line opened just before the Tokyo Olympics in 1964.

_____ **S.** At the time, the train ran between Tokyo and Osaka at speeds of 135 miles per hour.

_____ **T.** Now, the Shinkansen spans the island of Japan and can travel up to 185 miles per hour.

_____ **U.** Over 250 million people a year ride the Shinkansen, making it the most efficient and expedient mode of transportation in the country.

FivePoints
Learning

PARAGRAPH 5

England's Globe Theatre was built in 1599 and hosted several plays by William Shakespeare.

_____ Q. Shakespeare himself was part owner of the playhouse that held approximately 4,000 audience members.

_____ R. The original theatre was circular, but with a thatched roof covering three galleries.

_____ S. A replica of the Globe stands in London today and remains one of England's premier tourist attractions.

_____ T. The Globe was rebuilt but was then demolished shortly after England's Puritan laws forced the closure of all theatres.

_____ U. Sadly, the theatre burned to the ground in 1613, when a prop cannon ignited the thatched roof during a performance.

TEST NINE

PARAGRAPH 1

The first records of prosthetic limbs appeared in accounts from ancient Greece and Rome.

_____ **Q.** These early limbs were made of wood, metal, or iron and were both cumbersome and not very functional.

_____ **R.** Thanks to these technological advances, prosthetic limbs are more functional and versatile than ever before.

_____ **S.** Bionic limbs are fitted meticulously to the patient's body and help amputees carry on the lives to which they were accustomed before their injuries.

_____ **T.** Since then, scientists have made great strides in the development of prosthetic limbs.

_____ **U.** Modern limbs, often referred to as "bionic" limbs, are made from lighter and stronger materials like plastics and carbon-fiber composites.

PARAGRAPH 2

Everybody knows the alphabet but few know that it originated in the ancient civilizations of Sumer and Egypt.

_____ **Q.** The Cuneiform system, developed by the Sumerians, used a series of wedge-shaped marks pressed into clay while the Egyptians used hiero-glyphics.

_____ **R.** The English adopted the Latin alphabet in the Middle Ages, and it has since become the most widely used alphabet in the world.

_____ **S.** But the Phoenicians developed the first true alphabet, which consisted of 22 letters and inevitably spread to other cultures along their trade route.

_____ **T.** Then, the Roman Empire took the Greek system and developed it into the Latin alphabet.

_____ **U.** For example, the Greeks modified the Phoenician alphabet to include vowels.

FivePoints
Learning

PARAGRAPH 3

The teddy bear was named after President Theodore Roosevelt, the 26th president of the United States.

_____ **Q.** Mitchtom's toy was a best seller and teddy bear fever swept the nation.

_____ **R.** A cartoonist for the Washington Post depicted the event as the President holding a cute, cuddly little bear.

_____ **S.** The original teddy bear is now in the Smithsonian Institute for all to see.

_____ **T.** While on a hunting expedition, Roosevelt came across a bear cub and refused to shoot it.

_____ **U.** Morris Michtom saw the cartoon and began selling "Teddy's bears" at his candy store in Brooklyn, New York.

PARAGRAPH 4

Did you know that veterinarians often assist space programs all over the world?

_____ **Q.** Of course, veterinarians are also responsible for ensuring that the animals are healthy, correctly housed, and properly fed in space.

_____ **R.** The information gathered from these experiments is used to better understand the conditions of astronauts in space.

_____ **S.** For example, NASA employs veterinarians to work with their research teams.

_____ **T.** When they aren't caring for animals, they plan and conduct other experiments and present their findings to NASA officials.

_____ **U.** They help these teams conduct experiments on how animals are affected by zero gravity.

FivePoints
Learning

PARAGRAPH 5

Nomadic tribes inhabited Siberia until the Mongols overran the country in the early 1500's.

_____ **Q.** The Russians built fortresses throughout the territory in an effort to control this great expanse of land.

_____ **R.** Although the Russian government continues to encourage settlement in Siberia, its harsh environment has impeded development even to this day.

_____ **S.** However, Siberia wasn't populated at all until the completion of the Trans-Siberian Railway.

_____ **T.** Any regions that still weren't populated were used for political prisons during the reign of the Soviet Union.

_____ **U.** When the Mongol Empire fell apart, the Russian monarchy decided to explore the region.

FivePoints
Learning

TEST TEN

PARAGRAPH 1

The manatee is a gentle aquatic creature that roams the Caribbean Sea and the Coast of West Africa.

_____ **Q.** Like walruses, manatees have large, round bodies and thick wrinkled gray skin, yet their flippers and tail are distinct among underwater mammals.

_____ **R.** Manatees use their flippers to steer themselves through the water while their tales propel them at a slow pace.

_____ **S.** Although they look nothing like mermaids, manatees do closely resemble walruses.

_____ **T.** Unbelievably, these creatures were once confused for mermaids by sailors navigating these waters.

_____ **U.** However, their large tails can propel the manatee up to 20 miles per hour when frightened or threatened.

PARAGRAPH 2

Alcatraz Island was first called the Island of the Pelicans as it was covered by these birds when discovered.

_____ **Q.** After its discovery, Alcatraz served myriad functions over the years, starting with the construction of a military fortress.

_____ **R.** This fort was later used during the Civil War to protect against possible attacks from Confederate sympathizers.

_____ **S.** Later on, the army used it as a military prison before it eventually turned into a federal penitentiary.

_____ **T.** The penitentiary was shut down for good in the early 1970's and has served as a popular tourist attraction ever since.

_____ **U.** The fortress was built on top of the island to provide coastal defense for the new state of California during the Gold Rush.

FivePoints
Learning

PARAGRAPH 3

The African Wild Dogs of the Sahara are extremely efficient pack hunters, ranking them among the most notable predators of their kind.

_____ **Q.** That way, if their prey can run faster, the dogs let their victims become exhausted and therefore vulnerable.

_____ **R.** Their cooperative skills enable the pack to target and bring down larger animals such as antelopes and zebras.

_____ **S.** In addition, they can run an average of 35 m.p.h. for over 3 miles, but only in short bursts.

_____ **T.** Once they have an animal in sight, the wild dogs surround and trap their prey.

_____ **U.** This broad hunting style requires them to survive in large expanses, which many believe is the cause of their endangerment.

PARAGRAPH 4

Wassily Kandinsky is a Russian painter who is often credited as the founder of abstract art.

_____ **Q.** His work gained a following amongst art patrons who helped him create a new art movement called the Blue Rider group.

_____ **R.** At a young age, Kandinsky's love of music and paintings laid the groundwork for his artistic future.

_____ **S.** Kandinsky felt constrained by the paintings he studied and began experimenting with less structured methods of creating art.

_____ **T.** But he didn't actually study art until his thirties after becoming disenchanted with his life as a Law Professor.

_____ **U.** He spent his last years in a small town outside Paris where he painted until his death in 1944.

FivePoints
Learning

PARAGRAPH 5

The matryoshka, or "stacking doll," is emblematic of Russia's rich culture.

_____ **Q.** The most valued dolls tell stories whose roots are in Russian fairy tales.

_____ **R.** "Matryoshka" comes from the Latin root word "mater," meaning mother.

_____ **S.** Sometimes these figures are identical, but usually there is a slight difference in the coloring of the costumes.

_____ **T.** The mother doll pulls apart to reveal increasingly smaller dolls as each figure is opened.

_____ **U.** But these are more than just dolls, as many are over a century old and are considered highly valuable works of art.

FivePoints
Learning

—————— TEST ELEVEN

PARAGRAPH 1

The clownfish and the sea anemone rely on each other for survival.

_____ Q. Their relationship is "symbiotic" in that the benefits of both parties are mutual.

_____ R. Meanwhile, the clownfish helps the sea anemone by using its bright colors to lure other fish toward their poisonous tentacles.

_____ S. For instance, as the clownfish is immune to the sea anemone's poison, it can hide within its tentacles and avoid predatory fish.

_____ T. If it weren't for their symbiotic relationship, both the clownfish and the sea anemone would be endangered or even extinct.

_____ U. Once the sea anemone has eaten, the clownfish feasts upon the leftovers and cleans out the tentacles in the process.

PARAGRAPH 2

Frida Kahlo was a Mexican painter who lived from 1907 until 1954.

_____ Q. She began painting during this time of isolation using oils as her medium.

_____ R. These oil paintings helped introduce a modern form of folk art into Mexican culture.

_____ S. But when she suffered serious injuries from a bus accident, Kahlo spent a full year recovering in bed.

_____ T. She continued to paint for the remainder of her life, and her art would soon become famous throughout the world.

_____ U. She trained for three years at the National Preparatory School in Mexico to become a doctor.

FivePoints
Learning

PARAGRAPH 3

The city of Pompeii was covered in volcanic ash in 79 A.D after the eruption of Mount Vesuvius.

_____ **Q.** Pliny's writings enabled them to accurately reconstruct the daily life of Pompeii's people.

_____ **R.** Architects found that the volcanic remains preserved much of the city and its contents.

_____ **S.** It stayed covered until its discovery in the late 16th century.

_____ **T.** Therefore, visitors of the ancient city can take a rare look at the daily life of a person living in the Roman Empire.

_____ **U.** Historians also uncovered detailed writings by a Roman scribe named Pliny the Younger.

PARAGRAPH 4

Thomas Savery invented the steam engine in 1698.

_____ **Q.** Savery attempted to develop a more efficient way to drain water from coal mines rather than horse operated pulley systems.

_____ **R.** This machine consisted of a water tank which, when heated, produced steam that forced water out of the mine shaft.

_____ **S.** Afterwards, a cold water sprinkler cooled the steam and created a vacuum that sucked more water out of the mine shaft through a bottom valve.

_____ **T.** Savery's machine became a standard in technology until a more efficient model, the Newcomen Engine, was later invented.

_____ **U.** His original machine worked on the principle that water vapor takes up more space than its liquid form since their molecules are further apart.

PARAGRAPH 5

The Baobab tree stands 20 meters tall and reaches 15 meters in diameter, thereby dwarfing other vegetation in the African savannah.

_____ **Q.** But besides its unique appearance, the Baobab tree has many uses.

_____ **R.** Thus, several myths and legends formed about how this tree came to be planted in such an unusual manner.

_____ **S.** So enormous is the Baobab tree that when it sheds its leaves, the tree appears upside down with its roots reaching up towards the sky.

_____ **T.** The oldest of these enormous trees is over 2,000 years old.

_____ **U.** It is known as the Tree of Life because it provides shelter, food, and water to animals and people alike.

FivePoints
Learning

—— TEST TWELVE

PARAGRAPH 1

The tomb of Emperor Qin Shihuangdi, the first emperor of China, tells an odd story of preservation.

_____ **Q.** In addition, they come with wooden war chariots, full sized terra-cotta horses, and thousands of actual weapons.

_____ **R.** Later, archaeologists uncovered eight thousand of these soldiers near the Emperor's alleged tomb.

_____ **S.** So far, they have excavated over a thousand life-sized soldiers, each designed with unique characteristics.

_____ **T.** Some believe that the army was created to protect Emperor Qin in death, but we may never know for sure.

_____ **U.** It begins with farmers discovering the head of a soldier made of terracotta clay.

PARAGRAPH 2

The piano's long history began in the early 1700s when Bartolomeo Cristofori invented the pianoforte.

_____ **Q.** Cristofori was the keeper of instruments for the royal court, and he created the instrument to improve upon the sound of the harpsichord.

_____ **R.** The seven-octave piano is the most played instrument in the United States.

_____ **S.** The next change occurred as a result of the Industrial Revolution with development of high quality steel wire, thereby enhancing the piano's sound.

_____ **T.** Cristofori's piano made way for the invention of Johann Schmidt's upright piano.

_____ **U.** As the piano continued to evolve into its current form, the octave range expanded to a grand total of seven.

FivePoints
Learning

PARAGRAPH 3

Fibonacci is often considered the greatest mathematician of his era.

_____ **Q.** This search led to the discovery of the now-famous Fibonacci sequence.

_____ **R.** He discovered the system while traveling across Africa.

_____ **S.** As a child, Fibonacci excelled in algebra, geometry, and even trigonometry.

_____ **T.** Besides his scholarly work as a mathematician, Fibonacci also studied nature and searched for laws and patterns related to mathematics.

_____ **U.** His expertise in these subjects resulted in his replacing the Roman Numeral system with the Hindu-Arabic system.

PARAGRAPH 4

Totem poles are unique to the Native American tribes of the Pacific Northwest Coast.

_____ **Q.** They are elaborate pillars carved from the wood of cedar and spruce trees.

_____ **R.** The oldest totem poles were unable to survive the centuries, but their existence is confirmed in the accounts of early explorers.

_____ **S.** There are three types of totem poles: Crest totem poles, story-telling totem poles, and mortuary totem poles.

_____ **T.** The totem poles of today are primarily seen as art works.

_____ **U.** They can also be distinguished by color, schemes and symbols.

FivePoints
Learning

PARAGRAPH 5

Killer bees are man-made hybrids of the European honey bee and the African honey bee.

_____ **Q.** Some of these bees traveled North, and have slowly spread throughout Mexico and the Southern half of the United States.

_____ **R.** For example, the killer bee will attack for no apparent reason and react in great numbers to minor disturbances.

_____ **S.** One key distinction is that the killer bee is smaller than the typical European bee.

_____ **T.** A much more important difference, however, is in its temperament and behavior.

_____ **U.** Luckily, it can only sting once before dying, and its sting is no more powerful than that of the European bee.

—— TEST THIRTEEN

PARAGRAPH 1

Genghis Kahn was a powerful Mongolian leader who lived in the 1st century.

_____ **Q.** But Kahn was not satisfied with ruling just Mongolia and so embarked on a campaign to expand his territory.

_____ **R.** During the expansion, the people began calling him Kahn, meaning, "king."

_____ **S.** He then developed a code of laws called the yasa to rule the newly unified Mongolian empire.

_____ **T.** By the end of his reign, Genghis Kahn had taken possession of more territory than any other leader in history.

_____ **U.** His first order as a tribal leader was to unite all nomadic tribes under a single government.

PARAGRAPH 2

In 1984, the U.S. government proposed the idea for an International Space Station.

_____ **Q.** The completed station is the size of a soccer field, and several astronauts can indeed live and work on the space station at any given time.

_____ **R.** It also provides a neutral laboratory where scientists can conduct their research and collaborate in space.

_____ **S.** Each country is responsible for the running and the upkeep of the station.

_____ **T.** It wanted to provide a place where international scientists could live, work, and research in space.

_____ **U.** A total of fifteen countries became involved in the International Space Station Project.

FivePoints
Learning

PARAGRAPH 3

King Cobras are among the most feared snakes on the planet.

_____ **Q.** So venomous is the snake that one bite is enough to kill an elephant.

_____ **R.** Luckily, they prefer to stay away from humans unless they are cornered, so approach King Cobras at your own risk.

_____ **S.** Not only are they the longest of venomous snakes, but they are also some of the most deadly predators alive.

_____ **T.** Before striking, the King Cobra can rise up to a third of this great height before striking their victim with powerful venom.

_____ **U.** For one thing, King Cobras can weigh up to twenty pounds and reach lengths of up to eighteen feet.

PARAGRAPH 4

The Greek island Kalymnos is the center of the sponge diving industry.

_____ **Q.** Early on, divers used a flat stone called a skandalopetra in order to reach the bottom of the ocean.

_____ **R.** The divers would have to hold their breath as they used the skandalopetra to cut the sponges loose.

_____ **S.** Years later, diving suits that allowed for more time spent underwater were invented.

_____ **T.** Due to the invention of synthetic sponges, there are only a few of these divers left in the world.

_____ **U.** Sponges are aquatic animals that attach to the ocean bed before they are extracted and then used for bathing and household cleaning.

FivePoints
Learning

PARAGRAPH 5

The chocolate industry is full-time and is worth billions of dollars throughout the world.

_____ Q. These purple seeds are spread out and covered until they ferment and turn brown.

_____ R. Once large enough, colorful pods form along their edges, thereby making them ripe for harvesting.

_____ S. The pods are then split open with a machete so that the farmers can remove the seeds from the inside.

_____ T. Its humble beginnings are in the rainforests where cacao plants are grown on small family farms and plantations.

_____ U. Finally, they are collected and sent to chocolate companies where they are used to produce the candy we all enjoy so much.

FivePoints
Learning

—— TEST FOURTEEN

PARAGRAPH 1

In 1587, hundreds of people left England to establish the first settlement in America.

_____ **Q.** When White returned three years later, he found the settlement deserted.

_____ **R.** John White left with Fernandez, but promised his family that he would return with supplies.

_____ **S.** The colonists settled on an island off the coast of North Carolina, which they named, "Roanoke."

_____ **T.** Before a full investigation could take place, a hurricane forced White to leave Roanoke and the settlers were never located.

_____ **U.** Soon after, a sailor named Simon Fernandez returned to England.

PARAGRAPH 2

Monarch butterflies go through four stages of being during their life cycle.

_____ **Q.** The cocoon will remain a chrysalis for ten days until it undergoes a process called metamorphosis.

_____ **R.** Finally, a butterfly emerges from the cocoon and lays its own eggs to continue the life process.

_____ **S.** The process begins when monarch eggs are laid on milkweed plants; once the caterpillar larva hatches, it will feed on the milkweed below.

_____ **T.** Two weeks later, the larva develops into a full-grown caterpillar, which then looks for a stem so it can form a cocoon.

_____ **U.** In order to build a cocoon, the caterpillar uses silk to change into a chrysalis.

FivePoints
Learning

PARAGRAPH 3

During World War II, Allied forces needed a secret code that the Japanese could not decipher.

_____ **Q.** Johnston was given the approval to start a Navajo Code Talker unit, and the first group developed a code that could be communicated in seconds.

_____ **R.** These brave Navajo soldiers coded countless messages on the battlefield that helped the Allies win the war.

_____ **S.** This code used Navajo words and associated them with the military terms they resembled.

_____ **T.** The Navajo words were then spelled out according to letters in the English alphabet.

_____ **U.** Engineer Philip Johnston proposed the Navajo language because it has no alphabet.

PARAGRAPH 4

Edward Jenner created the smallpox vaccine — the world's first successful vaccine — in 1796.

_____ **Q.** Jenner developed the vaccine after repeated experiments in which he injected controlled doses of smallpox into healthy individuals.

_____ **R.** Scientists continued his work by developing vaccines to prevent polio, rubella, and measles.

_____ **S.** His experiments demonstrated that when exposed in small doses, the body's immune system would fight off the microbes that cause infectious diseases.

_____ **T.** Jenner's immunizations are among the most important medical achievements of all-time.

_____ **U.** The vaccinated subjects became immune and showed no sign of illness.

FivePoints
Learning

PARAGRAPH 5

Jose Gaspar was a fierce pirate who captured over 400 ships in 40 years before retiring at 65.

_____ **Q.** He escaped capture by jumping into the Gulf of Mexico, leaving behind $30 million of his captured treasure.

_____ **R.** He decided not to pass up the opportunity to seize one final treasure.

_____ **S.** The crew reportedly buried the treasure somewhere along Florida's Peace River, but the bounty remains undiscovered.

_____ **T.** A few hours after his announcing his retirement, Gaspar noticed a merchant ship sailing through nearby waters.

_____ **U.** Unfortunately, the ship turned out to be a U.S. Naval vessel, upon which Gaspar was arrested on the spot.

FivePoints
Learning

——— TEST FIFTEEN

PARAGRAPH 1

Light sticks provide a luminescent glow without the use of a bulb or a battery.

_____ **Q.** Their subsequent reaction causes an energy surplus by raising electrons to a higher level.

_____ **R.** Once the electrons return to their normal state, the energy produced becomes light.

_____ **S.** The two solutions within the stick then mix together.

_____ **T.** This glow is caused by a chemical reaction that occurs inside of the stick when it is snapped.

_____ **U.** This process is called chemiluminescence.

PARAGRAPH 2

One who wants to express something far away may use the phrase, "From here to Timbuktu."

_____ **Q.** Tuareg Imashagan, who needed a place to settle with his animals during the dry season, founded the city in the 11th century.

_____ **R.** Thanks to the miracle of trade, Timbuktu became a thriving center for culture and education.

_____ **S.** Timbuktu is an actual city located along the Sahara desert in Mali, Africa.

_____ **T.** This is largely due to the city's close proximity to the Niger River, which was crucial for the gold trade.

_____ **U.** Timbuktu flourished for centuries until France colonized West Africa in 1893.

FivePoints
Learning

PARAGRAPH 3

Poison dart frogs are located in the rainforests of Central and South America.

_____ **Q.** This is understandable as one frog contains enough poison to kill 10,000 men in a matter of minutes.

_____ **R.** Amerindian tribes will use its skin to secrete poison onto the tips of their arrows.

_____ **S.** "Poison dart" refers to the weapons used from the frog's poisonous skin.

_____ **T.** Therefore, when raised in captivity, none of these frogs are even remotely poisonous.

_____ **U.** The frogs attain their poisonous secretions by consuming rare insects in the wild.

PARAGRAPH 4

Captain Joshua Slocum was the first man to sail around the world alone.

_____ **Q.** Upon his return, Slocum wrote a book about his adventures called, *Sailing Alone Around the World*.

_____ **R.** He further challenged expectations by using lunar distance observation, considered by many an obsolete navigational method.

_____ **S.** The 46,000-mile voyage began in Boston, Massachusetts and ended three years later in Newport, Rhode Island.

_____ **T.** He achieved this on a 36-foot boat called the Spray.

_____ **U.** Instead of navigating with modern instruments, Slocum used dead reckoning to determine his longitude.

FivePoints
Learning

PARAGRAPH 5

China's Forbidden City housed the government of the Ming Dynasty.

_____ Q. The completed city contained 800 buildings, 9,000 rooms, and was divided into two courts.

_____ R. The Forbidden City is now a museum, providing us an insightful glimpse into China's textured past.

_____ S. Construction of the city took over 14 years to finish.

_____ T. A total of twenty-four emperors ruled within the Forbidden City until the abdication of Pu Yi, the last emperor of China.

_____ U. The royal family presided within the inner court and settled political affairs within the outer court.

——— TEST SIXTEEN

PARAGRAPH 1

Jacob and Wilhelm Grimm were born in Germany in the late 18th century.

_____ **Q.** They continued gathering stories throughout the country until they published the first edition of their book, *Children and Household Tales*.

_____ **R.** While studying law at the University of Marburg, the brothers collected folk and fairy tales from their fellow students.

_____ **S.** Without the book, classic stories such as *Snow White*, *Hansel and Gretel*, and *Little Red Riding Hood* may have vanished from history.

_____ **T.** Before the book was published, these stories were passed down through generations and survived orally.

_____ **U.** Their 6th and final edition of the book contained over 200 tales and is now a priceless representation of German culture.

PARAGRAPH 2

The Trans-Siberian Railroad was built during the reign of Tsar Alexander III and is the longest single rail system in Russia.

_____ **Q.** The completed railroad offers four different routes covering 5,787 miles and spans seven different time zones.

_____ **R.** The Trans-Siberian is the main route beginning in the capital city of Moscow to the West, and ending 5,000 miles later in the Eastern port of Vladivostok.

_____ **S.** Although it was built over a century ago, the railway remains essential to Russian transportation, as it's the only one that spans the entire country.

_____ **T.** Moreover, the engineers took 14 years to build it because they had to work from opposite ends and head towards the middle.

_____ **U.** In fact, the system is so long that a complete rail trip on the Trans-Siberian route would take a passenger eight days to complete.

FivePoints
Learning

PARAGRAPH 3

Earthquakes occur when the tectonic plates underneath the earth's surface shift apart or push into each other.

_____ Q. Meanwhile, earthquakes that occur in the ocean can spawn coast-shattering tsunamis.

_____ R. This is measured by the Richter scale, which rates earthquakes from a barely noticeable 1 to a powerful and devastating 10.

_____ S. Scientists are studying new ways to predict when and where an earthquake will come.

_____ T. Low-scoring earthquakes contain minor plate movements, yielding but a slight trembling of the ground above.

_____ U. However, high-scoring earthquakes yield such significant movements that entire buildings and even cities can be destroyed.

PARAGRAPH 4

St. Bernards were first bred in the late 17th century by a group of monks in the Swiss Alps.

_____ Q. These dogs were named for the Great St. Bernard's Pass, a 49-mile route that crossed through their monastery.

_____ R. The monks used their St. Bernards to locate people buried deep within the snow.

_____ S. Then, one would lie down on the traveler while another returned to the monastery for help.

_____ T. An Augustine monk founded the monastery to provide safety for travelers along the dangerous path.

_____ U. Over the next 150 years, these heroic dogs would save the lives of nearly 2,000 travelers.

FivePoints
Learning

PARAGRAPH 5

Clara Barton dedicated her life to helping those in need.

_____ **Q.** She became a teacher when she turned 17 and opened up a free school thereafter.

_____ **R.** Barton brought the Red Cross to America, became its President, and remained so for 22 years.

_____ **S.** When the war ended, Barton traveled to Europe and discovered the Red Cross organization.

_____ **T.** During the Civil War, Barton quit her teaching job to bring fresh supplies to soldiers and nurse others back to health.

_____ **U.** These acts of kindness inspired the nickname, "Angel of the Battlefield."

—— TEST SEVENTEEN

PARAGRAPH 1

The Leaning Tower of Pisa remains an everlasting example of superior Roman-esque architecture.

_____ **Q.** Nevertheless, experts predict the tower will stand safely for another 300 years.

_____ **R.** In 1999, for example, a British engineering professor devised a plan to remove ground from the high side of the tower to reduce the lean.

_____ **S.** The 187-foot tower always leaned significantly to the south and instantly became known for its awkward stance rather than its outward beauty.

_____ **T.** It was built on a riverbed of sand and clay that have slowly compressed the underlying ground over time.

_____ **U.** Many people worry the tower will eventually topple from its own weight.

PARAGRAPH 2

Search and Rescue (SAR) units use canines to track missing people.

_____ **Q.** They also undergo behavioral training so that they can work alongside other dogs and injured people.

_____ **R.** The journey begins with the SAR putting the dogs through a rigorous training process in which their agility and endurance are tested.

_____ **S.** Once the dogs are deemed mission ready, they join one of the 150 canine search units across the country.

_____ **T.** These amazing dogs are responsible for recovering lost children, disoriented hikers, and natural disaster victims.

_____ **U.** Both trainings take a year to complete, and most dogs begin their training when they are mere puppies.

FivePoints
Learning

PARAGRAPH 3

Louis Armstrong was born in New Orleans, the "Birthplace of Jazz," in 1901.

_____ **Q.** Oliver mentored the young Louis, who was soon performing on steamboats that traveled up and down the Mississippi River.

_____ **R.** Armstrong would later start his own band, and go on to become one of the most influential Jazz trumpeters of the 21st century.

_____ **S.** He left the steamboat jobs behind and headed for Chicago following an invitation from King Oliver to play with his band.

_____ **T.** Celebrity cornet player King Oliver was first to notice Armstrong's talent.

_____ **U.** When he was 11, Armstrong was sent to a home for troubled boys where he learned how to play the cornet.

PARAGRAPH 4

Lunar roving vehicles (LRV's) are specially designed to travel around the surface of the moon.

_____ **Q.** The original model, which closely resembled the modern-day dune buggy, aided astronauts in their lunar explorations.

_____ **R.** However, technology at the time limited the LRV's capabilities.

_____ **S.** These vehicles contained all the communication and research equipment necessary for NASA.

_____ **T.** Newer prototypes were later developed to better meet the requirements for extended missions.

_____ **U.** The latest LRV models tested at NASA's lunar simulation area use sand dunes to simulate a lunar environment and ensure they are ready for action.

PARAGRAPH 5

Waterspouts occur most commonly in tropical environments.

_____ **Q.** At this point, an invisible vortex reaches all the way from the surface of the ocean to the cloud above at wind speeds of over 40 miles per hour.

_____ **R.** During the next stage, a wind shift pours into a funnel and forms a cloud.

_____ **S.** The funnel itself reaches from the ocean and kicks up violent waves before weakening and dissipating.

_____ **T.** A spiral pattern of dark and light water then emerges from the spot.

_____ **U.** The first indication of a waterspout is a dark spot that forms on the ocean.

—— TEST EIGHTEEN

PARAGRAPH 1

The Black dragonfish is a sea creature living in the deep recesses of the ocean.

_____ **Q.** In addition, photophores are scattered along the dragonfish's body to further assist its sight.

_____ **R.** Like other deep-sea creatures, the dragonfish produces its own light through an appendage on its neck called a chin barbell.

_____ **S.** It resides 2,000 feet below the surface of the ocean with some of the most stalwart creatures under the sea.

_____ **T.** The dragonfish uses these features to lure in nearby prey.

_____ **U.** As their prey becomes attracted to the light of the barbell, they float right into their deadly jaws.

PARAGRAPH 2

King Tutankhamen is the most famous of all the Pharoahs buried in Egypt's Valley of the Kings.

_____ **Q.** After a five-year search, Howard Carver and Lord Carnarvon unearthed the burial chamber of the young King in 1922.

_____ **R.** When they entered the tomb, Carver and Carnarvon discovered a false room containing a hidden door that led to the main chamber.

_____ **S.** They struggled to find the tomb at first because it was buried by debris and surrounded by other tombs.

_____ **T.** They were shocked to discover that the chamber had not been looted and was in near-perfect condition.

_____ **U.** The unearthed relics currently travel the world and continue to fascinate history buffs of all ages.

FivePoints
Learning

PARAGRAPH 3

Rice, the staple food of over half of the world's population, is often grown using wet rice cultivation.

_____ **Q.** Next, excess chaff and dust are removed by shaking the rice back and forth on a basketwork tray.

_____ **R.** The newly harvested grains are then threshed using stones that separate the grains of rice from the surrounding husk.

_____ **S.** This process usually takes place in tropical or semi-tropical environments where the water is around three centimeters deep.

_____ **T.** Finally, the rice dries in the sun until it is ready to be hulled and polished before ultimately being sold and eaten.

_____ **U.** The rice is then planted in rows and is harvested a month after flowering.

PARAGRAPH 4

The Indian flying fox is one of the world's largest bats in the world.

_____ **Q.** These camps contain anywhere between several hundred to several thousand bats.

_____ **R.** As darkness approaches, they fly off in search of ripe fruit.

_____ **S.** Like other bats, Indian flying foxes roost upside-down in camps during the daytime.

_____ **T.** Due to their size, a group of flying foxes will often render an entire fruit tree bare before returning to their roosts.

_____ **U.** One bat-like feature is its four feet wide wingspan that enables the fox to fly and swim.

FivePoints
Learning

PARAGRAPH 5

While most vaults store valuables like gold or diamonds, one vault in Norway stores something altogether different.

_____ **Q.** Moreover, the Global Seed Vault secures seeds to assure the world has food for years to come.

_____ **R.** Its purpose is to guard these seeds and ensure they do not face extinction.

_____ **S.** This is not a new idea, as farmers have always saved seeds for the forthcoming harvesting seasons.

_____ **T.** But the seeds in the vaults are stored in airtight bags so that they will remain fertile in the coming year.

_____ **U.** The Svalbard Global Seed Vault stores plant seeds from each of the 1,400 seed banks located around the world.

——— TEST NINETEEN

PARAGRAPH 1

The electromagnetic spectrum refers to three types of light: ultraviolet, visible, and infrared.

_____ **Q.** All the colors in ROYGBIV are measured according to wavelengths of light.

_____ **R.** Of the three, the human eye can only see visible light, as it's made from the same colors of the rainbow.

_____ **S.** These colors — red, orange, yellow, green, blue, indigo, and violet — are often remembered using the acronym, ROYGBIV.

_____ **T.** However, white and black are the two extremes of the spectrum with white reflecting all of the colors and black absorbing them all.

_____ **U.** Red has the longest wavelength in the spectrum while violet has the shortest.

PARAGRAPH 2

The frigatebird is a unique species of seabird.

_____ **Q.** It is the size of a duck and inhabits tropical areas along the coast.

_____ **R.** Ironically for a seabird, the frigatebird is unable to swim because its feathers are not waterproof.

_____ **S.** These skills stem from its enormous wingspan of up to six feet

_____ **T.** Worse still, the species is barely able to walk due to its tiny feet.

_____ **U.** However, it makes up for these weaknesses with extraordinary flying skills and the ability to steal food from other birds in mid-air.

FivePoints
Learning

PARAGRAPH 3

The renowned poet Octavio Paz was born in Mexico City in 1914.

_____ **Q.** By the time he died, Octavio Paz had published a total of 40 books.

_____ **R.** Paz was later awarded the Nobel Prize for Literature in recognition of his work.

_____ **S.** He developed a love of literature at a young age, and even founded a literary magazine as a teenager.

_____ **T.** He then went on to publish his first book of poems, *Luna Silvestre*, and continued to write throughout his life.

_____ **U.** Paz's writings included themes of philosophy, art, politics, and religion.

PARAGRAPH 4

Palm Island, the world's largest artificial island, is shaped like a palm tree and resides off the coast of Dubai.

_____ **Q.** He designed the island like a palm tree to provide a unique beachfront property.

_____ **R.** The ruler of Dubai, Sheik Mohammed, developed the island to attract tourists and to keep up with the small country's rapid population growth.

_____ **S.** This island was not created by volcanoes or coral growth, but was actually man-made.

_____ **T.** Specifically, it is located in the Persian Gulf.

_____ **U.** As of today, Palm Island is projected to have a population of 120,000 residents in the next ten years.

FivePoints
Learning

PARAGRAPH 5

Scientists in England recently discovered that humans are not the only beings using antibiotics.

_____ **Q.** While studying these gardens, researchers also identified a new antibiotic that has the potential to treat human fungal infections.

_____ **R.** Moreover, they prevent unwanted fungi and bacteria from forming on the leafcutter ants' gardens.

_____ **S.** During a recent study, researchers found that leafcutter ants also produce antibiotics.

_____ **T.** The ants use them in the same way that humans use weed killer in gardens.

_____ **U.** Since the gardens are vulnerable to bacterial and fungal infections, the risk of depleting the food supply is massive.

—— TEST TWENTY

PARAGRAPH 1

Frank Lloyd Wright is considered one of the greatest architects of the 20th century.

_____ **Q.** Wright wanted architecture to reflect the spirit of democracy and other American values that he cherished so deeply.

_____ **R.** He was born just two years after the Civil War, at which time American architecture still reflected European aesthetics.

_____ **S.** The thousands of buildings that Wright designed would change the way Americans viewed architecture.

_____ **T.** He was also inspired by American landscapes and made sure to represent them in his works.

_____ **U.** These works included houses, museums, offices, churches, bridges, and even schools.

PARAGRAPH 2

Seeing-eye dogs are instrumental in providing a greater degree of freedom to the visually impaired.

_____ **Q.** Labrador Retrievers, German Shepherds, and Golden Retrievers are the most commonly chosen breeds for this line of work.

_____ **R.** These breeds begin training as soon as they are old enough to leave their mothers.

_____ **S.** Thus, the dogs are placed with permanent families for whom they provide an invaluable service for the rest of their lives.

_____ **T.** The dogs are then taught to assist the visually impaired with everyday activities like shopping, public transportation, and other errands.

_____ **U.** Within two years, the dogs are trained and mature enough to become faithful companions.

FivePoints
Learning

PARAGRAPH 3

Tornadoes can reach wind speeds of over 300 miles per hour.

_____ **Q.** Cold and warm air then combine together to form a funnel cloud, indicating that the tornado has finally taken shape.

_____ **R.** As the speed rises, the updraft changes the spinning effect from horizontal to vertical wind gusts.

_____ **S.** They are formed within thunderstorms when the wind changes direction and increases its speed, thereby creating a horizontal spinning effect.

_____ **T.** This effect occurs in the lower atmosphere and cannot be seen by the naked eye.

_____ **U.** At this point, the wind spreads through the storm at approximately 2-6 miles wide.

PARAGRAPH 4

While most plants need water to survive, Venus flytraps are actually carnivores.

_____ **Q.** These bizarre plants sprout up in areas that do not contain soil that is rich in nutrients.

_____ **R.** When the mouth opens, unsuspecting insects are attracted to the flytrap's trigger hairs.

_____ **S.** Therefore, they obtain their necessary nutrients from insects.

_____ **T.** If anything bends these hairs, the leaves of the trap close in a matter of seconds.

_____ **U.** The closed trap dissolves the insect with its digestive juices over a two-week period before reopening for its next meal.

FivePoints
Learning

PARAGRAPH 5

The Global Positioning Satellite (GPS) has replaced maps, landmarks, and stars as the most relied upon navigational method.

_____ Q. Once the receivers analyze radio signals from the satellites, they are finally able to calculate a traveler's exact location on earth.

_____ R. The GPS locates the available satellites and finds locations based on its projected distance using a process called trilateration.

_____ S. There are 27 of these satellites in space, each revolving around the earth twice a day with at least four satellites accessible at any given time.

_____ T. Each GPS is linked up to an extensive satellite network originally developed by the U.S. military.

_____ U. As the satellites' orbits can shift, the Department of Defense monitors their positions and sends tracking adjustments to GPS receivers.

FivePoints
Learning

Answers &
Explanations

ANSWERS & EXPLANATIONS: TEST ONE

Paragraph 1 (SQTUR)

The topic sentence explains that Yuri Gagarin was born before space travel was a reality. S states that he grew up to become a cosmonaut, and Q follows with Gagarin becoming the first human to orbit the Earth. T provides the name of the spacecraft he traveled in, and explains that it contained two compartments. U follows to describe the contents of each section. R concludes the paragraph with Gagarin reentering the atmosphere as a hero.

Paragraph 2 (QUTSR)

The topic sentence introduces the lure of the legend of El Dorado. Sentence Q expands on the geography of the city as well as the legend itself. U introduces the explorers and adventurers who searched for the city. T refers to the efforts discussed in U as fruitless, but states that the origin of this legend is based partially on fact. S then describes the tribe on which these tales were based. R concludes the paragraph by explaining that the term El Dorado is now a figurative term used to denote a dream or desire.

Paragraph 3 (QRUTS)

The topic sentence states that the lionfish is causing extensive damage to the marine ecosystem in the waters off of South Florida. Q states that the lionfish was accidently released into these waters. R continues, explaining that since it has no enemies in these waters, the population has exploded. U describes this fish as an invasive predator that preys upon native fish. T explains that this has upset the balance of the ecosystem. S concludes the paragraph by stating that scientists are searching for ways to eliminate the lionfish and bring the ecosystem back into balance.

Paragraph 4 (RUTSQ)

The topic sentence states that an orchestra conductor has many important jobs. R gives the first of a conductor's many jobs, which is to recruit musicians. The next three sentences describe the work associated with the musical pieces themselves. U must come after R because it leads with, "The conductor also..." T follows referring back to U with the word "these," referring to the musical pieces

FivePoints
Learning

in T. S then states that they must know when each instrument enters the musical works discussed in U and T. Q summarizes all of the conductor's jobs, thereby wrapping the paragraph up.

Paragraph 5 (UTSQR)

The topic sentence states that the World Cup is one of the most popular sporting events in the world. U explains the purpose of this event. T then gives the date of the first World Cup. S then states that only 13 teams participated in the first tournament but that number has increased to 32. Q leads with, "Of these teams..." and says that only eight have won the world cup. R concludes with the statement that the World Cup unites the world by promoting fair play and respect among its nations.

ANSWERS & EXPLANATIONS: TEST TWO

Paragraph 1 (SRUQT)

The topic sentence states that ants communicate using chemicals. S then provides the name of this communication method. R then states that ants secrete their own chemicals called pheromones and goes on to explain how they are used. U gives further information regarding the scent's uses, and Q follows with the final reasons as proven by the phrase, "Ants also use this scent..." Finally, T summarizes the importance of this means of communication.

Paragraph 2 (QSUTR)

The topic sentence defines viruses. Q then follows to explain that viruses are made of nucleic acids. S goes on to describe the protein that protects these viruses. U then states that a liquid membrane surrounds the protein, which is used to attach the virus to a host cell. T describes how the host cells replicate. R wraps up the paragraph by stating that this replication causes a viral infection.

Paragraph 3 (QSURT)

The topic sentence introduces Grandma Moses. Q follows describing the humble beginnings of her work. The next three sentences describe Grandma Moses' subsequent rise to fame. S introduces Louis Caldor who bought her collection from the store. U says that Caldor showcased her works at the Museum of Modern Art. R states that she became a household name soon after. T concludes the paragraph by naming her as one of the most famous American folk artists of the 20th century.

Paragraph 4 (TRSUQ)
The topic sentence introduces the need for an efficient way to provide clean water in Ancient Rome. T provides the solution to this problem: The aqueduct. The next three sentences describe how the aqueducts are designed. R explains that the aqueducts relied on gravity to transport the water and were therefore designed with slopes. S then explains that each slope had to be just right to keep the water flowing. U adds the caveat that some aqueducts were built below ground as well as above, which made it more difficult to get that exact slope each time. Q concludes the paragraph by explaining that these aqueducts were used until the fall of the Roman Empire.

Paragraph 5 (STRQU)
The topic sentence defines the Internet. S explains that no one owns the Internet as a whole. T follows with an example of one of those pieces. R states that since no one owns it, it is governed by rules called protocols. Q then describes the organizations that monitor these protocols. U then concludes the paragraph with the statement that the experts in each group do their part to maintain the integrity of the Internet.

ANSWERS & EXPLANATIONS: TEST THREE

Paragraph 1 (SRUQT)
The topic sentence introduces Mark Twain. The next three sentences are written in chronological order. S gives his date of birth. R states that he left school at 12 to become a printer's apprentice. U discusses his next career as a river pilot's apprentice, and introduces the "Mark Twain" penname. Q has Twain going back to writing when the river trade slowed down. T completes the paragraph providing the number of books he wrote and naming his lasting achievements.

FivePoints
Learning

Paragraph 2 (RQSTU)

The topic states that domestic pigs become feral when released into the wild. R defines the word feral. Q follows and explains that the ability to turn feral is called phenotypic plasticity. S describes the first changes that occur as the pig becomes feral. T offers a few more significant chances, while U concludes with a comparison between the feral pig and the domestic pig.

Paragraph 3 (UTRSQ)

The topic sentence introduces the Hanging Gardens of Babylon built by King Nebuchadnezzar II. U explains that these gardens were built to comfort the king's homesick wife. T then explains why she was homesick. The next three sentences describe the gardens. R refers back to the queen mentioned in T so it must come first in the explanation. S then explains how the levels were held up. Q concludes the paragraph by stating that the final structure became one of the Seven Wonders of the Ancient World.

Paragraph 4 (QURTS)

The topic sentence introduces Benjamin Banneker and establishes the order of accomplishments as discussed in the preceding sentences. The remaining sentences maintain this order by follow basic chronology. Q states that he was first recognized as a scientist after he correctly predicted a solar eclipse. U describes how he then helped map the boundaries of the capital city. R follows logically as it discusses the almanac while T elaborates further on the Almanac writing. S concludes the paragraph by adding a final thought on Banneker's legacy.

Paragraph 5 (UQRTS)

The topic sentence defines aquaponics. U elaborates on the initial definition with more of a description of how it works. The rest of the paragraphs describe the aquaponic cycle. Q states that the cycle begins with fish and R explains that their waste fertilizes the water. T explains that the plants then remove the nutrients from the water. S concludes with the process beginning once again.

FivePoints
Learning

ANSWERS & EXPLANATIONS: TEST FOUR

Paragraph 1 (QSURT)

The topic sentence introduces the stiletto snake. Sentence Q follows explaining that the snake's name relates to its fangs. S elaborates further on the fangs and the role they play in the snake's attacks. U then describes the attack itself. R explains why this attack method is useful while T concludes with the fangs returning to their neutral, horizontal position.

Paragraph 2 (QTUSR)

The given sentence introduces the Bering Land Bridge as one of the world's ancient crossroads. Q follows with the origin of its name. The next three sentences explain how it came to be. T discusses the last ice age and its role in the bridge's making. U continues by stating that this drop created a 1,000-mile wide stretch of land that linked Asia and North America. S then finishes the explanation with the migration of the masses to North America. R concludes with the fact that anthropologists continue to study the area.

Paragraph 3 (RUSTQ)

The topic sentence introduces Atlantis and its origins. R describes the island and how it was allegedly destroyed. U changes gears by explaining a possible misunderstanding in the translation of the tale. S introduces the subject of satellite images of Spain. T posits that these images resemble the structures described in the legend. Q then concludes the paragraph by stating that the Atlantis mystery may soon be solved.

Paragraph 4 (SRUTQ)

The topic sentence introduces the samurai warrior of Japan. S provides their purpose, which was to protect the feudal lords. R then defines the code that governed their actions and how it related to their way of life. U states that the first samurai were archers. T follows with the phrase "in addition," and adds more information as to how they fought. Q ends the paragraph with the end of the samurai.

Paragraph 5 (RTSUQ)

The topic sentence defines hurricanes. The five detail sentences R gives their alternate name and states they can reach speeds of up to 185mph. T continues

FivePoints
Learning

leading with, "They can also…" and describes the swells hurricanes can cause in the ocean. S transitions into a discussion on the hurricane season. U states that meteorologists watch tropical storms carefully during the season. Q comes to the conclusion that they have plenty of time to warn us of imminent hurricanes.

ANSWERS & EXPLANATIONS: TEST FIVE

Paragraph 1 (QRSUT)
The topic sentence concerns the origins of the New York Stock Exchange. Q follows by establishing the basic rules to govern the Exchange. R states that the Exchange would be located on a specific street. S confirms that it was Wall Street and explains how Wall Street got its name. U gives the reason that the wall was built. T concludes the paragraph with news that the wall is no longer there.

Paragraph 2 (STRQU)
The topic sentence introduces the Mexican revolutionary Pancho Villa. S is next and describes his early life. T and R explain why he became a revolutionary leader. T must come first as it clearly introduces Abraham Gonzalez whereas R merely refers to him. Q then states he became the best-known leader of the Mexican Revolution. U concludes the paragraph with Villa's assassination.

Paragraph 3 (SQTUR)
The topic sentence states that great herds of buffalo once roamed the American West. S explains how Buffalo came to be in America. Q then discusses how Native Americans only hunted what they needed for their tribes. This is contrasted in T in which the white settlers hunted buffalo for profit. U gives the grim effect of the excessive hunting. R concludes by stating that scientists are trying to rebuild the buffalo nation from the few survivors.

Paragraph 4 (QSRTU)
The topic sentence explains the purpose of the North Pole Environmental Observatory. Q establishes when the study begins and what specifically is studied. S follows to explain what information they need to record. R is next because it explains one method that the scientists use for their records. T then offers up additional information on the complicated research process. U concludes the paragraph by summarizing the importance of the research.

Paragraph 5 (QUTSR)

The topic sentence introduces the Colossus of Rhodes and offers up a brief back-story. Q picks up from where the back-story of Demetrius' retreat left off and explains where all the material came from. U follows with the name the sculptor who created this great statue. T then describes how he made the statue to stand upright. S follows with the unfortunate defeat of the statue by an earthquake, and R concludes by telling us how invaders stole and sold the pieces of the Colossus after the crash.

ANSWERS & EXPLANATIONS: TEST SIX

Paragraph 1 (UQRST)

The topic sentence introduces Mount Everest as the tallest mountain in the world. U gives the mountain's original name, while Q provides George Everest as the reason for the name change. R discusses the demand for new measurements while S shows that the demand was eventually met. T ends the paragraph with the recalculated height of Mount Everest.

Paragraph 2 (TRQSU)

The topic sentence discusses the Age of Exploration and the role of Spain's conquistadors. T introduces one such conquistador, Juan Ponce de Leon. R gives a little background on his exploring history with Columbus before he set out on his own. Q follows with Ponce de Leon's major discovery and governing of Puerto Rico. S then states that De Leon returned to Florida after his term as governor. U ends the paragraph as the journey turns out to be his last.

Paragraph 3 (RQSUT)

The topic sentence introduces the sport of geocaching, and the tools needed to participate in this activity. R follows the topic sentence because it tells where to find grid coordinates how difficult they are to locate. Next is Q, which explains the purpose of these difficulty levels. S has the appropriate location chosen, and the remaining sentences discuss the hunt itself. U explains what to do when the geocache and logbook are found. Finally, T discusses logbook procedure and where to place the geocache once the logbook has been signed.

FivePoints
Learning

Paragraph 4 (QTUSR)

The topic sentence provides the definition of origami. Next is Q with an explanation of the importance of origami in Japanese culture. T follows by restating the importance of origami, and providing the reason that its use was limited. U goes on to explain how that changed with the introduction of the book **Window on Midwinter** with S offering up the details associated with the book. R ends the paragraph by summarizing the positive effect it had on the accessibility of origami.

Paragraph 5 (TUQRS)

The topic sentence states that Khufu's Great Pyramid is the most famous of all Ancient Egyptian pyramids. T qualifies the topic sentence by stating that it's one of the current Wonders of the World due to its size and architectural genius. The order of ideas dictates that a sentence on size must come first. In this case, it is U. Q leads into the architectural genius reason and then describes the manpower used to build the pyramid. R then gives the specific details of the required manpower to build the pyramid. S concludes by restating the pyramid's greatness, and its ability to continue to awe visitors to this day.

ANSWERS & EXPLANATIONS: TEST SEVEN

Paragraph 1 (QRSUT)

The topic sentence introduces the time in which period barn raisings were common. Q then elaborates on the necessity of barn raisings during this time period. R follows as it addresses the concerns of the families alluded to in Q. S explains that everyone in the community was required to collaborate on the job, while U offers up the effects of the collaborative efforts. T concludes the paragraph by summarizing its purpose and importance.

Paragraph 2 (UQRST)

The topic sentence introduces cowboy Nat Love. U begins by stating that Love was freed from slavery at the end of the Civil War. Q then talks about his first job at a ranch once he was a free man. R is next because it explains that he was working at the Duval Ranch when he was given the name, "Deadwood Dick." S then explains how he got that name. T concludes the paragraph with a tribute to Nate Love's cowboy spirit.

FivePoints
Learning

Paragraph 3 (RUTSQ)

The topic sentence introduces the leafy seadragon. R then states that it's actually a type of seahorse. U follows with their alternate name, the "Australian Seahorse." Next is T, describing the seadragon's appendages. S then explains the purpose of these appendages. Q concludes to explain that the Australian government protects the leafy seadragon.

Paragraph 4 (TRSUQ)

The topic sentence introduces the catapult. T then states the function of the weapon and how it works. R follows by defining how the effects of the catapult are achieved. Next is S, which describes the basket and the counterweight that are used on opposite ends of each arm. U follows by explaining how the projectile is finally launched. Q ends the paragraph by explaining why it is no longer used.

Paragraph 5 (SRQTU)

The topic sentence defines the Supreme Court in the context of the U.S. government. S is first because it describes it origins and its purpose. R then offers up an additional purpose. Next, Q gives the number of these constitutional cases that are ruled on each year by the Supreme Court. T then says that the nine permanent justices decide upon these cases. U then concludes by explaining that the Supreme Court is the last court that can be appealed to.

ANSWERS & EXPLANATIONS: TEST EIGHT

Paragraph 1 (QSRUT)

The topic sentence introduces the first space-based optical telescope and gives its size and weight. Q then gives the name of the telescope and elaborates further on the size and weight. S adds an extra fact to the Q sentence on how the telescope works. R has to follow because it digresses from the above sentences by discussing the first collected image. U directly contrasts R with the number of images regularly captured today. This leaves T to conclude the paragraph with the fact that the telescope provides invaluable information about our solar system.

FivePoints
Learning

Paragraph 2 (QURTS)

The topic establishes the platypus as a unique mammal. Q follows with the major distinction that it lays eggs. U continues by listing other unique features. R summarizes the features by indicating that they enable navigation on land and water. T digresses into a discussion on the platypus' venomous qualities, and S concludes with an example of how they use venom for defense and offense.

Paragraph 3 (RUTSQ)

The topic sentence explains that Alexander the Great was schooled by Aristotle. R is next, stating that this education prepared him to become one of the greatest conquerors of all time. U further explains that it didn't take long after Alexander's schooling for him to become a captain of the Macedonian army. T follows with the fact that he gained the respect of his soldiers as captain. S indicates Alexander's transition from captain to king. Q concludes the paragraph by listing his conquests and his death.

Paragraph 4 (RSTQU)

The topic sentence introduces the bullet train of Japan as the first high speed train in the world. R follows as it discusses the first incarnation of the train. S discusses its maximum speed rate while T contrasts with its current rate. Q adds more information about the train's current form, while U concludes the paragraph by stating its continued efficiency and popularity.

Paragraph 5 (QRUTS)

The topic sentence introduces the Globe theatre as well as playwright William Shakespeare. Q then offers more information on Shakespeare's role. R describes the original theatre and the thatched roof that covered it. U changes gears with the theatre's untimely destruction. T follows by describing its reconstruction and subsequent demolition. S ends the paragraph by declaring the Globe replica a popular tourist attraction today.

FivePoints
Learning

ANSWERS & EXPLANATIONS: TEST NINE

Paragraph 1 (QTUSR)

The topic sentence describes the origins of prosthetic limbs. Q follows to explain how they were originally made. T then indicates that the way these limbs are constructed has changed. U follows by elaborating on their current make-up and introduces the term "bionic limbs." S then explains how these bionic limbs have improved the lives of their recipients. R concludes the paragraph explaining that these technological advancements have helped prosthetic limbs come a long way since their early beginnings.

Paragraph 2 (QSUTR)

The topic sentence states that the alphabet originated in Sumer and Egypt. Q elaborates on the alphabets of the civilizations mentioned in the topic sentence. S transitions into the first true alphabet and how it evolved from culture to culture. U addresses how the Greeks added vowels to the alphabet. T then explains how the Romans adapted the Greek system into what is now known as the Latin alphabet. R concludes with the English adopting the Latin alphabet, which would subsequently become the most widely used alphabet in the world.

Paragraph 3 (TRUQS)

The topic sentence explains that the teddy bear was named after President Theodore Roosevelt. T explains they story from which the teddy bear was inspired. R states that a cartoonist depicted this story in cartoon form. U goes on to explain that this illustration inspired the creation of the first teddy bear. Q then states that teddy bear fever soon swept the nation. S concludes by saying that the original bear is in the Smithsonian for all to see.

Paragraph 4 (SUQTR)

The topic sentence asks if you knew that some veterinarians work with astronauts. S follows with the example that NASA employs them for to assist their research teams. U follows to explain how the veterinarians help these teams with their animal research. Q acknowledges that veterinarians still care for animals during their time at NASA. T addresses the other experiments they conduct when they aren't tending their veterinary needs. R concludes by the uses of the information gathered.

FivePoints
Learning

Paragraph 5 (UQSTR)

The topic sentence introduces Siberia and describes its conditions before the Mongols came in. U then states that the Russians took control of the land after the Mongolian Empire fell apart. Q discusses how the Russians used the new land to build fortresses throughout. S transitions into the fact that no one lived in Siberia until the completion of the Trans-Siberian Railroad. T elaborates on the population theme by explaining that prisoners made up all the non-populated regions. R concludes that Siberia remains largely barren despite Russia's efforts to encourage settlement over the years.

ANSWERS & EXPLANATIONS: TEST TEN

Paragraph 1 (TSQRU)

The topic sentence introduces the manatee and lists the bodies of water in which it can be found. T follows by stating that, "unbelievably," these creatures were once confused for mermaids. S elaborates that manatees look more like walruses than mermaids. Q follows by introducing a comparison between walruses and manatees involving flippers and tails. R goes on to explain how these flippers and tail are used for swimming, albeit at a slow pace. Finally, U must follow because it offers a contrast with the slow pacing mentioned in R.

Paragraph 2 (QURST)

The topic sentence addresses Alcatraz Island and its discovery. Q introduces its many uses post-discovery and kicks off the paragraph with its use as a military fortress. U then describes the construction of the fortress, while R addresses its use during the Civil War. S explains its later use as military prison and then as a federal penitentiary. T concludes by describing its current draw as a state park.

Paragraph 3 (RTSQU)

The topic sentence describes African Wild Dogs of the African Sahara as efficient pack hunters and notable predators. The following four sentences describe how the packs hunt their prey. R begins by explaining that the pack hunting style mentioned in the topic sentence allows them to track and bring down much larger prey. T describes how the pack surrounds and closes in on the animals listed in

FivePoints
Learning

R. S then elaborates on the dogs' ability to run at a consistent speed for up to 3 miles, while Q explains the benefits of this running method. The final sentence is U, which restates the efficiency of their hunting style.

Paragraph 4 (RTSQU)

The topic sentence introduces artist Wassily Kandinsky as the founder of abstract art. R explains his background that led him towards a life of art. T follows to tell of his decision to formally study art after beginning a career in Law. S describes his experience at art school and his move away from formal painting as he developed his own style. Q goes on to explain that this unique style gained a following and in turn spurred an art movement. U ends with his last years in France where he continued to paint for the remainder of his life.

Paragraph 5 (RTSUQ)

The topic sentence introduces the matryoshka dolls of Russia. R then gives the meaning of the word as "mother." T follows to describe how the figures fit together. S continues with a description of their unique physical characteristics. U then states that they are highly prized art forms. Q concludes with a description of the most highly prized of all matryoshka dolls.

ANSWERS & EXPLANATIONS: TEST ELEVEN

Paragraph 1 (QSRUT)

The topic sentence describes the relationship between the clownfish and the sea anemone. Q follows to define this relationship as symbiotic and explains what this term means. S discusses how the clownfish benefits, while R does the same for the sea anemone (Look out for the transitional phrases, "for instance" and "meanwhile.") R also introduces the sea anemone's tentacles, which are elaborated upon in sentence U. T gives a concluding thought on what would happen if these two creatures didn't work together.

Paragraph 2 (USQRT)

The topic sentence introduces the painter Frida Kahlo. U describes her original intentions to become a doctor, and S then explains why her schooling was cut short. Q states that she began to paint during this bed-ridden time. R then

FivePoints
Learning

describes these paintings and indicates their future influence. T concludes the paragraph by explaining that she continued to paint for the remainder of her life.

Paragraph 3 (SRUQT)

The topic sentence describes the volcanic eruption that covered the ancient city of Pompeii. S states that the city remained hidden until its discovery in the 16th century. R explains that the volcanic ash had preserved the city perfectly, while U introduces additional writings that historians unearthed. Q follows by stating that these writings allowed archeologists to accurately reconstruct daily life in Pompeii. T concludes by explaining Pompeii's appeal.

Paragraph 4 (QURST)

The topic sentence introduces Thomas Savery as the inventor of the steam engine. Q explains Savery's purpose in designing the engine. U explains the scientific principle upon which "the original machine" worked. R and S explain how the machine actually operated on the basis of this scientific principle: R describes how the water was raised by fire and then S describes how the vacuum sucked even more water out of the mine shaft. T concludes the paragraph by stating that Savery's model continued to be used until the invention of a more efficient model.

Paragraph 5 (TSRQU)

The topic sentence describes the size of the Baobab tree of Africa. T restates the enormity of the tree and S further elaborates on its size while discussing its unusual appearance. R explains that its appearance has resulted in myths about the tree. Q changes the subject to the tree's usefulness, while U elaborates that it's called "the tree of life" due to how useful it is.

ANSWERS & EXPLANATIONS: TEST TWELVE

Paragraph 1 (URSQT)

The topic sentence introduces Emperor Qin Shihuangdi and establishes the paragraph's preservation theme. U begins the story with the discovery of a soldier made from terracotta clay in farmland. Next is R, with archeologists discovering even more soldiers. S provides the total number of clay soldiers that they found

FivePoints
Learning

and addresses their unique characteristics. Q leads with "In addition…" and adds the objects that accompany the soldiers. T then gives a possible explanation for why the army was created but leaves the door open for other answers.

Paragraph 2 (QTSUR)

The topic sentence gives us the name of the original piano as well as its creator, Bartolomeo Cristofori. Q sets up the conditions that led to Cristofori inventing the pianoforte, while T transitions from Cristofori's version to that of Johann Schmidt. S leads with "The next change…" and describes the evolution of the piano's strings. U indicates the accumulation of the piano's seven-octave range, and finally, R concludes by stating that the seven-octave piano is the most played instrument in the United States.

Paragraph 3 (SURTQ)

The topic sentence introduces Fibonacci as the greatest mathematician of his time. S then gives an overview of his mathematical strengths at an early age. U indicates that his strengths in math led to his replacing of the Roman numeral system with the Hindu-Arabic system. R tells us where he found the number system. T transitions from his scholarly accomplishments to his interest in mathematics in nature. Q ends with this interest eventually leading to his discovery of the Fibonacci sequence.

Paragraph 4 (QRSUT)

The topic sentence explains that totem poles are unique to the Pacific Northwest Coast. Q then defines what totem poles actually are. Next, R provides the reason that the earliest totem poles are no longer with us. S changes gears into the totem poles of today by listing the three types. U follows by stating that these poles have distinct visual styles. T concludes with the fact that contemporary poles are made as works of art.

Paragraph 5 (QSTRU)

The topic sentence explains the origins of Africanized honey bees. Q explains how these bees came about in North and South America. S compares their appearance to their hybrid ancestors, while T offers up the distinction of their temperament and behavior. R gives an example of the temperament and behavior and U concludes the paragraph by reassuring the reader about the power of their sting.

FivePoints
Learning

ANSWERS & EXPLANATIONS: TEST THIRTEEN

Paragraph 1 (USQRT)

The topic sentence introduces Genghis Kahn. U must follow as it provides his first order of business, which was to unite all the tribes under one government. S transitions into the laws that he decreed for this newly formed government. Q tells of his desire for expansion while R confirms that he was crowned "Kahn" as a result of the expansion process. T wraps up the paragraph with the reach of Genghis Kahn's empire towards the end of his reign.

Paragraph 2 (TUSQR)

The topic sentence introduces the U.S. government conjuring up the idea for a space station. T follows with the intended goal of the space station's development. U then states that 15 other countries joined the U.S. in this endeavor. S elaborates on the roles of all the countries involved in the station's management. S tells that the space station is now completed, and R concludes the paragraph by stating that it is fully operational.

Paragraph 3 (UTQSR)

The topic sentence introduces the King Cobra as the most feared and venomous snake on the planet. Sentence U follows because it mentions its size and its jumping capabilities as reasons for its fearsome reputation. T addresses exactly how far it can jump and then introduces its poisonous venom. Q then describes their venom in more detail. S concludes that it is among the deadliest predators alive, and R ends with the warning that it will only strike when it has been cornered.

Paragraph 4 (UQRST)

The topic sentence introduces the Greek island Kalymnos as the epicenter of the sponge diving industry. Q defines what a sponge actually is. Q talks about the early days of sponge diving and how it worked. R elaborates on the divers during this time. S transitions into a later time in which diving suits were used. T concludes with the fact that very few sponge divers still exist.

FivePoints
Learning

Paragraph 5 (TRSQU)

The topic sentence introduces chocolate as an industry. T explains that chocolate originates from plants in rainforests. R introduces the pods that form along the plants and how they enable harvesting. S then talks about how the pods are split open to extract the seeds used for chocolate. Q addresses the next stage for the seeds and U ends the paragraph with the seeds traveling to chocolate factories.

ANSWERS & EXPLANATIONS: TEST FOURTEEN

Paragraph 1 (SURQT)

The topic sentence introduces the first English Settlement in America. S then tells us exactly where they settled. U explains that Simon Fernandez had to return to England and R elaborates that Fernandez brought John White with him to get supplies. Q informs us that when White returned to Roanoke, all the settlers had mysteriously disappeared. T gives the tragic reason that White was never able to find the settlers that included his family.

Paragraph 2 (STUQR)

The topic sentence states that Monarch butterflies go through four stages during their life cycle. S addresses the start of the cycle with eggs hatching into caterpillar larva. T follows with the larva developing into a full-grown caterpillar. U then describes how the caterpillar uses silk to change into a chrysalis. Q then explains that it goes through metamorphosis during the following 10 days. R concludes with the butterfly emerging and laying more eggs so the cycle can begin again.

Paragraph 3 (UQSTR)

The topic sentence tells about the need for a code during World War II that the Japanese could not decipher. U follows with Phillip Johnson's recommendation that they use the Navajo language. Q continues with the approval of his idea and the development of the Navajo Code Talker unit. S explains how Navajo words were actually used, while T addresses how words could also be spelled out by way of the English alphabet. R concludes by summarizing the positive impact that this code and these soldiers had towards ending the war.

FivePoints
Learning

Paragraph 4 (QSURT)

The topic sentence introduces Edward Jenner and his developing of the smallpox vaccine. Q tells of the experiments that led to the vaccine, S describes the effects of the experiments, and U concludes that the experiments indeed worked. R then discusses how scientists have continued Jenner's work with developing vaccines, and T wraps up the paragraph by declaring Jenner's work among the most important medical achievements of all-time.

Paragraph 5 (TRUQS)

The topic sentence introduces the pirate Jose Gaspar as well as his retirement. T states he spotted a merchant ship within hours of announcing the retirement, while R explains he couldn't resist one more siege. But U offers up the twist that it was actually a U.S. Naval vessel, upon which Gaspar was arrested. Q follows with Gaspar's escape as well as his abandoning of the treasure. S concludes the paragraph by stating that this treasure was allegedly buried and has never been found.

ANSWERS & EXPLANATIONS: TEST FIFTEEN

Paragraph 1 (TSQRU)

The topic sentence introduces light sticks and summarizes how they work. T starts to explain the chemical reaction that results in the glow. S continues along with the chemicals actually mixing together. Q addresses the energy that results from the mixture. R then has the energy yielding the glow addressed in the topic sentence. Finally, U concludes by giving the entire process a name.

Paragraph 2 (SQTRU)

The topic sentence introduces the common phrase, "From here to Timbuktu." Q affirms the fact that Timbuktu is a real place. Q then tells us who founded the city and why. Next, T explains how its location made it a significant trading port. R continues to discuss the prosperity that thenceforth ensued. Finally, U concludes with the French colonizing Timbuktu.

Paragraph 3 (SRQUT)

The topic sentence introduces the poison dart frog. S explains what "poison dart" means. R then elaborates on how this poison is used for the weaponry introduced in S. Q is next as it affirms just how deadly the poison is. U then states that these frogs are not poisonous when kept in captivity, and T concludes by explaining why.

Paragraph 4 (STURQ)

The topic sentence introduces Captain Joshua Slocum as the first man to sail around the world on a solo mission. S follows and gives the length of his voyage as well as how long it took to complete. T then connects with, "He accomplished this feat…" and gives the size and name of his boat. R adds a fact about his bold navigational conquest, and Q concludes with Slocum writing a book about his adventures upon his return home.

Paragraph 5 (SQUTR)

The topic sentence introduces the Forbidden City and explains what it was. S then tells us how long it took to create. Q follows with the now-completed city and describes its structure. U then elaborates on its structure, specifically the two courts introduced in Q. T brings us to the end of the Forbidden City as a place of government, and R transitions into its current incarnation as a museum.

ANSWERS & EXPLANATIONS: TEST SIXTEEN

Paragraph 1 (RQTSU)

The topic sentence introduces the Grimm brothers and when they lived. R follows with the brothers collecting folk and fairy tales from their classmates in college. Q has them collecting more stories until their first book was published. T explains that there was no written record of these stories up until the book, while S offers some examples of stories that may have been lost without it. U wraps up the paragraph with their sixth and final edition of the book as well as its significance in German culture.

FivePoints
Learning

Paragraph 2 (UTQRS)

The topic sentence introduces the Trans-Siberian Railroad as the longest one in Russia. U elaborates that the railroad is so long that the completed trip takes 8 days. T states the number of years it took to complete as another example of its length. Q has the railroad now complete and provides yet more information on the railroad's enormity. R then gives the names and locations of the starting and ending stations of the completed railroad. S concludes by stating that it remains an important means of transportation in Russia today.

Paragraph 3 (RTUQS)

The topic sentence tells us how earthquakes occur. R then introduces the Richter scale and explains how it measures the earthquake process. Next, T and U describe the effects of both low and high-scoring earthquakes, respectively. Q transitions into what happens when an earthquake occurs in the ocean. S concludes the paragraph by stating that scientists are researching new ways to predict earthquakes.

Paragraph 4 (QTRSU)

The topic sentence introduces St. Bernards and their history. Q explains where the name comes from and establishes the route that crossed through the monastery in which they were bred. T establishes the area as unsafe and therefore the monastery's necessity as a shelter for travelers. R describes the St. Bernards' excellent sense of smell and how they use this sense to locate people buried in the snow. S then tells how they would then lie down on the traveler while another dog returned for help. U concludes with the number of travelers that the dogs have saved over the years.

Paragraph 5 (QTUSR)

The topic sentence introduces Clara Barton as a woman who dedicated her entire life to helping others. Q describes her earliest experiences helping others as a schoolteacher. T has Barton quitting her teaching job to help the wounded of the Civil War. U elaborates on her role in the Civil War as superintendent of Union nurses. S then introduces her work with the Red Cross after the Civil War. R concludes the paragraph with Barton bringing the Red Cross to America and presiding over it for many years.

FivePoints
Learning

ANSWERS & EXPLANATIONS: TEST SEVENTEEN

Paragraph 1 (STURQ)

The topic sentence introduces the leaning tower of Pisa. S explains how it became known as the leaning tower while T then explains exactly why it leans. Next, U addresses the concern that the tower will one day collapse. R offers an example of how this problem was addressed, and Q concludes with the reassurance that the tower will stand for a few more centuries.

Paragraph 2 (TRQUS)

The topic sentence introduces the use of canines in search and rescue units. T follows to state their purpose within these units. R then establishes the beginnings of their training. Next, Q transitions from their physical training to that of their social training. U then states that the training begins when the animals are merely puppies. S concludes the paragraph by explaining that, when their training is complete, the dogs are tested before finally joining a SAR unit.

Paragraph 3 (UTQSR)

The topic sentence introduces Louis Armstrong. U sets up his interest in music at an early age. T states that he kept his interest going before meeting up with cornet player King Oliver. Q has Oliver mentoring Armstrong before the latter would eventually find work playing on steamboats. Next up is S, with Armstrong leaving the steamboats to join Oliver's band. R concludes the paragraph with Armstrong starting his own band only to become one of the most beloved jazz musicians in history.

Paragraph 4 (QSRTU)

The topic sentence introduces lunar roving vehicles. Q follows by providing the function of the original model. S further elaborates on these vehicles and how they worked. R goes on to explain that its abilities were limited due to the technology at the time. T then describes the new prototype, and U ends with the testing of the new models to ensure that they are mission ready.

FivePoints
Learning

Paragraph 5 (UTRQS)

The topic sentence introduces the waterspout as a predominately tropical occurrence. U offers up the first indication that a waterspout is beginning to form. T follows by stating that a spiral water pattern begins to emerge from the dark spot discussed in U. R then describes the next stage with the wind forming a cloud, Q illustrates the vortex that connects to the cloud, and S ends the paragraph by summarizing the end of the waterspout.

ANSWERS & EXPLANATIONS: TEST EIGHTEEN

Paragraph 1 (SRTUQ)

The topic sentence introduces the black dragonfish as an aquatic creature that lives in the deep recesses of the ocean. Sentence S follows by explaining just how deep these recesses are. R compares it to other deep-sea creatures by explaining that the dragonfish can make its own light. T introduces its method of luring in prey while U provides more information on the subject. Finally, Q explains just one more way that dragonfish produces light.

Paragraph 2 (QSRTU)

The topic sentence introduces King Tutankhamen as well as where he was buried. Q follows by stating that Howard Carver and Lord Carnarvon searched five years before locating the tomb. S then explains why this mission took so long. R describes the false room that they discovered upon entering the tomb. T then describes the main chamber into which the hidden door mentioned in R led. U then concludes the paragraph by explaining what is now done with the relics found in the tomb.

Paragraph 3 (SURQT)

The topic sentence introduces wet rice cultivation. S begins the process describing how the soil is prepared with U discussing how it is planted and harvested. R transitions from harvesting to threshing. Next, Q talks about the next step for preparing the rice, and T wraps up the paragraph with the final steps before the rice is sold and eaten.

FivePoints
Learning

Paragraph 4 (USQRT)

The topic sentence introduces the Indian flying fox as one of the world's largest bats in the world. U describes its wingspan, a notable bat-like feature. S adds the additional bat-like quality of roosting in camps during the day. Q then states the number of foxes in the average camp. R has the flying fox searching for food come nightfall. T concludes the paragraph the foxes devouring all the food that they need before returning to their camps.

Paragraph 5 (URSTQ)

The topic sentence introduces a vault in Norway that does not store money. U gives it a name – the Global Seed Vault – and elaborates on it further. R tells us the purpose of the vault. S explains that this purpose is nothing new and discusses its origins in farming. T provides a contrast between the seeds in the vault and the seeds from the old farming days. Finally, Q concludes the paragraph by explaining that the Svalbard Global Seed Vault ensures the further supply of global food for years to come.

ANSWERS & EXPLANATIONS: TEST NINETEEN

Paragraph 1 (RSQUT)

The topic sentence introduces the three types of light referred to by the electromagnetic spectrum. R refers back to all three but then focuses on visible light. S lists out all the colors individually and organizes them into the acronym, ROYGBIV. Q then states that these colors are measured by wavelengths. Next, U mentions the colors with the longest and shortest wavelengths, respectively. T concludes the paragraph by explaining that white and black are the two extremes of the visible spectrum.

Paragraph 2 (QRTUS)

The topic sentence introduces the frigate as a unique species of seabird. Q then describes its size as well as its habitat. R then contrasts its reputation as a seabird with the fact that it can't swim. T adds an additional handicap in the form of their tiny feet. U then explains that they make up for these weaknesses with their exceptional flying ability. S finishes off with an explanation of why these birds are such exceptional fliers.

Paragraph 3 (STURQ)

The topic sentence introduces the poet Octavio Paz. S describes his early love of literature that led him to found a literary magazine. T follows because "he then went on" to write his first book of poetry. U elaborates on the themes of these poems. R is next with him winning the Nobel Prize in Literature as a result of his writing. Q concludes the paragraph with his death by which time he had written 40 books.

Paragraph 4 (TSRQU)

The topic sentence introduces Palm Island, brands it an artificial island, and gives its approximate location. T must follow as it gives Palm Island the specific location of the Persian Gulf. S then restates the fact that the island is artificial but substitutes the term "man-made" instead. R follows with the reasons that Sheik Mohammed created it. Q then explains the reason behind how he designed its shape. U concludes the paragraph by giving the projected population of the island when all the available real estate has been sold.

Paragraph 5 (STRUQ)

The topic sentence informs the reader that beings other than humans use antibiotics. S follows as it reveals that leafcutter ants also use antibiotics. T comes next with an analogy between the way humans use them and the way ants use them. R elaborates on this analogy by explaining why the ants are doing this. U offers evidence for the claims made in R, and Q concludes with the reveal that scientists, in studying the operations listed out in previous sentences, have discovered new antibiotics that may be useful for humans.

ANSWERS & EXPLANATIONS: TEST TWENTY

Paragraph 1 (RQTUS)

The topic sentence introduces the architect Frank Lloyd Wright. R provides the context for American architecture before Wright pursued this career. Q follows by introducing Wright's desire to capture the American spirit in his work as opposed to the European-influenced buildings mentioned in R. T must come next as it adds the influence of American nature. Then, U lists examples of the works mentioned in T. S concludes the paragraph with a summary of Wright's entire career.

Paragraph 2 (QRTUS)

The topic sentence states the purpose of seeing-eye dogs. Q then lists the breeds used for this purpose. R brings us to the beginning with their training as puppies. T follows as it goes into the training in more detail. U jumps ahead two years with the dogs fully trained, and S has the dogs meeting their owners and aiding them for the rest of their lives.

Paragraph 3 (STRUQ)

The topic sentence defines tornados. S explains that tornadoes start out as thunderstorms and then describes the horizontal spinning effect that occurs within their formation. T states that this spinning cannot be seen with the naked eye. R follows to explain how the updraft from rising air changes the horizontal spinning, discussed in S, to vertical. U states that the wind spreads through the storm, thereby resulting in the formation of the tornado, which is described in Q.

Paragraph 4 (QSRTU)

The topic sentence establishes the Venus flytrap as a plant that happens to be a carnivore. Q explains why it is a carnivore, and S confirms that they must obtain their nutrients from insects instead. R describes how flytraps catch these insects; T explains how the trigger hairs mentioned in R contribute to the process. U concludes with the plants digesting their food and reopening for the next meal.

Paragraph 5 (TSURQ)

The topic sentence states that the GPS has replaced traditional navigational methods. T informs the reader that each GPS is linked up to a satellite network. S follows as it explains how these satellites revolve around the earth and why that's important for every GPS system. Next, U states that the U.S. Department of Defense closely monitors these orbits for their accuracy. R then describes how the GPS uses the satellites to calculate their necessary locations, and Q ends the paragraph with the satellites linking the devices up with the traveler's exact spot on Earth.

FivePoints
Learning

INDEX

FivePoints
Learning